TWENTIETH CENTURY
INTERPRETATIONS
MAYNARD MACK, *Series Editor*
Yale University

NOW AVAILABLE
Collections of Critical Essays
ON

THE ADVENTURES OF HUCKLEBERRY FINN

ALL FOR LOVE

THE FROGS

THE GREAT GATSBY

HAMLET

HENRY V

THE ICEMAN COMETH

SAMSON AGONISTES

THE SOUND AND THE FURY

TWELFTH NIGHT

WALDEN

THE WASTE LAND

A
COLLECTION
OF
CRITICAL
ESSAYS

on "The Waste Land"

TWENTIETH CENTURY INTERPRETATIONS

A
COLLECTION
OF
CRITICAL
ESSAYS
on "The Waste Land"

Edited by
JAY MARTIN

Prentice-Hall, Inc.   *Englewood Cliffs, N.J.*

A SPECTRUM BOOK

Current printing (last number):
10 9 8 7 6 5 4 3 2

Contents

PART TWO—*Essays*

TWENTIETH CENTURY INTERPRETATIONS

A
COLLECTION
OF
CRITICAL
ESSAYS

on "The Waste Land"

T. S. Eliot's *The Waste Land*[1]

by Jay Martin

I

The publication of *The Waste Land* was the culmination for T. S. Eliot of several years of change in his personal life and a rapid development of responsiveness in his intellect and imagination. The grandson of the Reverend William Greenleaf Eliot, who had settled in St. Louis in 1834, and who subsequently founded Washington University, Eliot was born on September 26, 1888. As a child he spent his winters in St. Louis and his summers on the Massachusetts coast, whence his grandfather had come and to which, even earlier, his ancestor Andrew Eliot had immigrated from East Coker, England. "I perceived," Eliot wrote in 1928, "that I myself had always been a New Englander in the Southwest and a South Westerner in New England." He was also to be a British citizen and inheritor of the traditions of European literature—deeply attracted to English and European literature at Harvard, and intensely aware (like Henry James) of his American affiliations while in England—and ultimately, as Delmore Schwartz has well said, the International Hero.[2]

Eliot prepared for Harvard at Smith Academy in St. Louis (1898–1905), then at Milton Academy in Massachusetts (1905–1906). After three years, during which he published nine poems in the *Harvard Advocate,* he earned his A.B. He early showed a talent for putting himself in touch with people and ideas particularly important for the

[1] For advice in the preparation of this essay, I am indebted to Professors Maynard Mack, Norman Holmes Pearson, John C. Pope, and W. K. Wimsatt, who all read it in earlier drafts. I wish to dedicate my own contribution to this volume to Conrad Aiken, whose spirit pervades it, since he first taught me to understand modern poetry and introduced me to Eliot's achievement.

[2] Asked whether his poetic sensibility was connected with or derived from "the American past," Eliot responded, with appropriately Jamesian ambiguity: "Yes, but I couldn't put it any more definitely than that, you see. It wouldn't be what it is, and I imagine it wouldn't be so good; putting it as modestly as I can, it wouldn't be what it is if I had been born in England, and it wouldn't be what it is if I'd stayed in America. It's a combination of things."

consciousness of the modern world. At Harvard he not only read Donne's *Poems* and Arthur Symons's *The Symbolist Movement in Literature,* books which he said changed the whole history of his imagination; he also studied with Irving Babbitt and made friends with Conrad Aiken. After a year of graduate work in philosophy at Harvard, for which he received an M.A. degree in 1910, he went to Paris, where he was tutored by Alain-Fournier at the Sorbonne and attended the lectures of Henri Bergson at the University of Paris. Following out the lines opened to him by Symons and Babbitt earlier, he now read Gide, Claudel, and the French Symbolist poets. In the three years following (1911–1914) he studied again at Harvard, first with Josiah Royce and then with Bertrand Russell.

Actually and imaginatively, he was traveling the great circle from America to Europe and back. This was in the American tradition. Later nineteenth century American writers had established their careers as American travelers to Europe: Howells with *Venetian Life,* James with *Transatlantic Sketches,* and Twain with *Innocents Abroad*—the first books of each. And Eliot's contemporaries, no less, were finding what James called "a thicker civility" in Europe and England: Aiken, Pound, John Gould Fletcher, and H. D. were only a few of those established abroad by 1914. Ezra Pound, writing of Eliot in particular, really expressed the general sense which these writers all shared when he said: "London may not be the *Paradiso Terrestrae,* but it is at least some centuries nearer it than is St. Louis." In more general terms, Eliot himself later described his sense of culture and poetry in America at this time:

> Whatever may have been the literary scene in America between the beginning of the century and the year 1914, it remains in my mind a complete blank. I cannot remember a single poet of that period whose work I read. . . . Undergraduates at Harvard in my time read the English poets of the '90s, who were dead: that was as near as we could get to any living tradition. Nor can I remember any English poets then alive who contributed to my own education. . . . There were, in the early years of the century, a few good poets writing in England, but I did not know of their existence until later. . . . I do not think it too sweeping to say that there was no poet, in either country, who would have been of use to a beginner in 1908. The only recourse was to poetry of another age and to poetry of another language.

Eliot's Paradiso would necessarily be in Europe, in another country and another time.

Apparently he thought first of settling in Germany; but after spending the summer of 1914 on a Harvard traveling fellowship at Marburg, he was forced out of Germany by the beginning of the First World War, and inevitably went to England, where he remained, eventually to become a British citizen in 1927. There, through Pound, he came to know Yeats, Joyce, and Wyndham Lewis, among others. In 1915 he had his first publication outside of school magazines, "The Love Song of J. Alfred Prufrock," in *Poetry;* completed his dissertation for Harvard, on *Experience and the Objects of Knowledge in the Philosophy of F. H. Bradley,* but decided not to return to America to take his doctoral examinations in defense of his thesis; married, and began teaching, first at the High Wycombe Grammar School and later at the Highgate School. In succeeding years he reviewed books for literary, political, and philosophical journals. He became an assistant editor of the *Egoist* in 1917; in that year he also began working for Lloyd's bank, saw *Prufrock and Other Observations* through the press; and continued to write poetry. Between 1917 and 1920 he published, in all, three books of verse and two of prose. In 1921 he became London correspondent for *The Dial* and was making plans to begin, as editor, the magazine which would be called *The Criterion.*

Not surprisingly, by late 1921, this expense of energy had ended in exhaustion. He was forced to take a three months' leave of absence from the bank for a recuperation in Lausanne, Switzerland. Here he wrote out his first version of *The Waste Land.* It is impossible to say what part Eliot's physical depletion played in the composition of the poem. In a note to an essay included in this volume Conrad Aiken discusses some of its biographical background and suggests that Eliot's sudden release from an older verse tradition, his recent close reading of Dante, and a violent self-anger were the elements which combined explosively in its generation. To these we might add his attentive study of Pound's *Cantos,* a new application of Yeats's accomplishments in verse, and an awakening of his sense of the mythic method through his reading of Joyce's *Ulysses.* American writers, often defining originality as the product of the unconscious, had long shown an interest in dulling the consciousness, through exhaustion or alcohol, in order to allow the repressed subterranean springs of poetic genius to flow forth. Their symbolic value would be, as Eliot said of *Huckleberry Finn,* "all the more powerful for being uncalculated and unconscious." The tales of Poe, the origin (as Hawthorne describes it in "The Custom House") of *The Scarlet Letter,* the mental depression of Dreiser preceding the writing of *Sister Carrie,* and Stephen Crane's rapid compositions are all instances of a tradition to which Eliot may have responded, encouraging his emotions to overflow not in tranquility, but in a chaos of irresolution and daring, hesitation and precipitateness, depression and exaltation. Like these, *The Waste Land* is alive with the imaginative energy and fierce complexity of its genesis. For whatever reasons, Eliot's imagination was vividly open to the possibilities of language during the autumn and winter of 1921–1922.

The poem seems to have been composed rapidly. Before February 1922 Eliot had shown a completed typescript to Pound—"the manuscript of a sprawling chaotic poem," Eliot termed it in 1946. On February 22, Pound makes the first known mention of *The Waste Land* in a letter. "Eliot produced a fine poem (19 pages) during his enforced vacation," he writes, "but has since relapsed. I wish something could be found for him, to get him out of Lloyd's bank." Even this early, Pound was using Eliot's poem in his campaign to establish an annual supporting fund for deserving writers, the first of whom would, he hoped, be Eliot. He returns to the same theme several times. In March, for example: "Eliot, in bank makes £500. Too tired to write, broke down; during convalescence in Switzerland did *Waste Land,* a masterpiece; one of the most important 19 pages in English." Not long after, he expresses this view fully in an article called "Credit and the Fine Arts" in *The New Age:* "Rightly or wrongly some of us consider Eliot's employment in a bank the worst waste in contemporary literature. During his recent three months' absence due to a complete physical breakdown he produced a very important sequence of poems: one of the few things in contemporary literature to which one can ascribe permanent value."

Pound had by this time given the poem a concise new shape—he was engaged in helping Eliot work out the continuity (which Eliot seems always to have intended) in what he had regarded at first as merely a "sequence of poems." From the beginning of Eliot's manuscript, Pound eliminated a completed, 73–line poem, "Gerontion," which Eliot was using as a preface, and he persuaded Eliot to remove a prefatory quotation ("The horror! The horror!") from Conrad's *Heart of Darkness.* From the end of the poem he removed some scattered poems which Eliot had placed after what is now the conclusion. In general, he emphasized more strongly than Eliot had the essential continuity between the large structural units of the poem, by eliminating the obvious transitional, connective material which the poem had contained. By the time it left Pound's hands the poem had been reduced to about half of its original length. In acknowledgment of this "irrefutable evidence of Pound's critical genius," Eliot added to the poem the dedication "for Ezra Pound / il miglior fabbro" in the 1925 edition of his *Poems*.

But it was Eliot's genius which gave the poem its excitement, and the shape which it finally took was apparently implicit in its original form. Precisely what kind of poem this final one is critics have been attempting to say for more than forty years. As the reviewer for the *Times Literary Supplement* pointed out on the occasion of the publication of the authorized edition of the poem in 1961, the large and still growing body of critical discussion of the poem has been strangely inconclusive. What the poem is "about"; whether its form is new or old; what degree of coherency it possesses; the validity of its "method"; what influence, if any, for good or ill, it has had upon other poetry; its "place" in Eliot's career—these are general questions for which no generally accepted answers have been given. Even on the question of what kind of "belief" Eliot advocates or seeks to intimate in the poem there is wide disagreement: it has been seen as divorced from beliefs; as a stage on Eliot's way toward acceptance of Christianity or as deeply pessimistic, even nihilistic; as a satire with moral purposes or as utterly scornful of all possibility for improvement in human society; as a glorification of the past, expressing a sense that the knowledge of history brings freedom, or as a condemnation of the past waste lands culminating in the present one, and hence as expressing the idea that history is circular and teaches the defeat of man.

The reception of the poem after its earliest English and American appearances—in the first issue of Eliot's new magazine, *The Criterion*, for October 1922 and in *The Dial* for November 1922—suggests the diversity of response which the poem has ever since occasioned. Critics like Conrad Aiken, Gilbert Seldes, and Edmund Wilson greeted the poem with enthusiasm, and E. M. Forster found it so remarkably clear as to provide a "key as to what is puzzling in [Eliot's] prose"; others, however, suggested that it was a hoax, and Amy Lowell declared flatly: "I think it is a piece of tripe." [3] Only slightly more moderate, Louis Untermeyer wrote: "It is doubtful whether *The Waste Land* is anything but a set of separate poems, a piece of literary carpentry, scholarly joiner's work, the flotsam and jetsam of desiccated culture." It was, he concluded, a "pompous parade of erudition."

---

[3] Amy Lowell concluded by speaking of the poet himself scornfully: "Tom Eliot— he was brought up around here—is distantly related to the Harvard Eliots. But Tom is an intellectual and an intellectual cannot write a poem, which is a matter of heart and emotion."

On the careers of several poets contemporary with Eliot, the publication of the poem had decisive effects. Hart Crane asked Gorham Munson almost immediately after the American publication of *The Waste Land:* "What do you think of Eliot's *The Waste Land?* I was rather disappointed. It was good, of course, but so damned dead." For the next eight years he dedicated himself to writing *The Bridge,* which he saw as a powerful counteragent to what he considered the negativism of Eliot's poem. Sharing many of Hart Crane's assumptions about the nature of the American epic, William Carlos Williams remarked retrospectively in his *Autobiography* that *The Waste Land* was "the great catastrophe to our letters," and in his turn moved toward the composition of *Paterson.* Malcolm Cowley, in *Exiles' Return,* perhaps best put the case against Eliot:

> When *The Waste Land* first appeared, we were confronted with a dilemma. . . . We were prepared fervently to defend it against the attacks of people who didn't understand what Eliot was trying to do—but we made private reservations. . . . At heart—not intellectually, but in a purely emotional fashion—we didn't like it. We didn't agree with the idea that the poem set forth.

Even Eliot's admirers have been in disagreement about the qualities for which the poem should be praised. Edmund Wilson speaks of it as "simply one triumph after another," but understands the poem as a statement of profound disillusionment, while Helen Gardner maintains that it is actually "an *Inferno* which looked towards a *Purgatorio*" and perhaps a Paradiso. Critical of both these views, and following out the logic of some of Eliot's own critical pronouncements on James and Dante, I. A. Richards has argued persuasively that *The Waste Land* is a poem effecting "a complete severance between . . . poetry and all beliefs." Concerning the principles of its organization, its use of myth, and the nature and extent of its unity, there has been as wide a divergence of opinion.

II

I want to suggest now some of the ways in which the poem may be approached. So striking is Eliot's use of myth, so prominent his allusions, that critics have written largely of this aspect of his work, to the neglect of other possibilities. This is surely not to say that the "mythical" method, if it may be called such, does not hold a prominent, even a central place in the poem. Eliot himself, no doubt consciously, called attention to this element in his discussion of *Ulysses,* in *The Dial,* exactly one year after the appearance of *The Waste Land* in the same magazine.

> I hold this book [*Ulysses*] to be the most important expression which the present age has found. . . . In using the myth, in manipulating a continuous parallel between contemporaneity and antiquity, Mr. Joyce is pursuing a method which others must pursue after him. They will not be imitators any more than the scientist who uses the discoveries of an Einstein in pursuing his own, independent, further investigations. It is simply a way of controlling, of ordering, of giving a shape and significance to the intense panorama of futility and anarchy which is contemporary history. . . . It is a method for which the horoscope is auspicious. Psychology . . . ethnology, and *The Golden Bough* have concurred to make possible what was impossible even a few years ago. Instead of narrative method we may now use the mythical method. It is, I seriously believe, a step towards making the modern world possible for art, towards . . . order and form.

Where history appears so disordered, the poetic backward glance may give meaning to the present, which becomes significant through the realization of what has been destroyed or lost in it. In this sense, the mythical method is basically satirical. It provides the author with a point of view and a set of standards which give power to his invective and tragic weight to his criticism. At the same time, Eliot indicates—in the myth of the Fisher King, in the sterile societies chastised by prophets, in the social and moral chaos of the Middle Ages and Renaissance—that the waste land is an ever-present dimension of civilization. In this second sense, the backward glance into history provides him with a possible structure for a poem—one based not on contrast but on similarity. In the complex similarities between all times, in a point of view emphasizing the circularity of history, he finds both irony and hope. His apprehension of history is so neutral that he can escape the apparent decadence of the present and imagine a revived future.

The power of the poem to lead the reader into tradition—into myth, literature, philosophy, and religion—can be seen in the abundance of critical commentary which it has attracted. No other modern poem gives its readers quite so effectively the exhilaration needed to solve its difficulties. The nickname Old Possum, which Pound gave to Eliot, alludes to the opossum's ability to fade into the background. While the poem is obviously, on one level, a deep personal expression of Eliot's tastes, attitudes, and knowledge, on another, by his apparently impersonal surrender to tradition in his use of the mythical method, Eliot minimizes the evidence of his own creativity, in order to demand creativity of his reader.

Clearly Eliot used myth as much to give his poem an intelligible historical structure as to provide a point of view for satire. It was a device giving form and clarity to Eliot's view of modern life. He was not, he has made clear, attempting to speak for a "lost generation," or to express (as C. M. Bowra has claimed) the "reaction and defeat which followed the high hopes raised by the idealism of Woodrow Wilson." Eliot himself has commented: "I dislike the word 'generation.' When I wrote a poem called *The Waste Land* some of the more approving critics said that I had expressed 'the disillusionment of a generation,' which is nonsense. I may have expressed for them their own illusion of being disillusioned, but that did not form part of my intention." His intention was simply to write a poem which would confront the modern world by "giving a shape" to the anarchy which contemporary history seems to be.

The poem is, first of all, an experiment with language, the forging of a new poetic instrument with which one may be able to talk about the world, and so, by talking, order it. Like Joyce, Pound, Aiken, and Yeats, Eliot inherited the assumption of Flaubert and the French Symbolists that language easily decays into imprecision, "the slimy mud of words . . ./Approximate thoughts and feelings"; but that words are essentially regenerative, and that in the work of the artist there may spring forth "the perfect order of speech, and the beauty of incantation." The poet would purify the language of the tribe by giving it perfection, and thus power, in his art. Eliot follows Mallarmé's "L'art pour tous" in making this claim in his later "The Three Voices of Poetry," and defends the explorations of language which all of these writers had conducted:

> If you complain that a poet is obscure, and apparently ignoring you, the reader, or that he is speaking only to a limited circle of initiates from which you are excluded—remember that what he may have been trying to do, was to put something into words which could not be said in any other way, and therefore in a language which may be worth the trouble of learning.

In *The Waste Land* Eliot did not substitute the tag ends of past kinds of speech for his own speech, as if to imply that present day speech was useless; on the contrary, he demonstrated how alive and resounding with possibility current speech could be by his ability to incorporate into it fragments which had been long inert. He gave new relevance to both past and present by bringing the old and new powerfully together.

George Santayana once explained to William Lyon Phelps the weakness in American poetry around 1900 by suggesting that for American poets of that period the traditions of Transcendentalism or Brahmanism had been enfeebled by rapid change, leaving them with no vital background of value or belief which they shared with their audience. Even more accurate was Henry Adams's analysis in his *Life of George Cabot Lodge* (1911). Lodge, Adams says, could only assert his "suppressed instinct" for poetry in "a reaction against society." He was "talking and singing in a vacuum that allowed no echo to return."

From all that had been left out of "Tradition" by the poets and critics of the Victorian Twilight—the leaving out of which had led to the enfeeblement of their work—Eliot made his tradition. As personal, social, and historical life had seemed to become uglier, the Poets of Ideality had become all the more refined. Now, in the French poets Eliot saw "the poetical possibilities of the more sordid aspects of the modern metropolis, the possibility of fusion between the sordidly realistic and the phantasmagoric, the possibility of juxtaposition of the matter-of-fact and the fantastic and that the source of new poetry might be found in what had been regarded as the impossible, the sterile, the intractable, unpoetic." From the metaphysical poets and from such theologians as Lancelot Andrewes, he learned to restore to the poetic imagination a state of consciousness easily accommodating paradox, and thus to use his sordid new subjects in combination with the overrefined preoccupations of Ideality. The application of this technique is perhaps most obvious in lines which refer to both Webster and Baudelaire:

> "That corpse you planted last year in your garden,
> "Has it begun to sprout? Will it bloom this year?
> "Or has the sudden frost disturbed its bed?
> "Oh keep the Dog far hence, that's friend to men,
> "Or with his nails he'll dig it up again!
> "You! hypocrite lecteur!—mon semblable,—mon frère!"

He thus made a poetry which, as he said in *The Use of Poetry and the Use of Criticism,* "fuses the old and the obliterated and the trite, the current and the new and the surprising, the most ancient and the most civilized mentality." [4] Finally, he learned from Dante (although

---

[4] He was aware, too, of the Metaphysicals' emphasis on the word: "Andrewes," he said, "takes a word and derives the World from it."

doubtless from others too) that myth and ritual were ways of ordering moral and imaginative passion and might be used as symbols
whereby to reveal it.

These elements were already present in American culture. An
American, Stuart Merrill, was one of Mallarmé's intimates, and his
poems (in French) were published along with those of the Symbolist
group. Symons's book, so important for Eliot, was first published in
an American magazine. The poetry of the metaphysicals had attracted continuous interest in New England—Emily Dickinson, for instance, had read Donne carefully, and the first modern edition of
Donne published anywhere was edited by James Russell Lowell for
the Grolier Club in Cambridge. Dante scholarship, of course, had
long flourished at Harvard under the influence of Longfellow and
Charles Eliot Norton. But these remained largely unrealized elements
of power in the consciousness of Eliot's time until he made a modern
poetry from them.

Eliot restored to poetry, and renewed for the uses of the imagination, elements of strength in the English tradition which later nineteenth century poets had excised from their verse. He freely employed
wit, broad humor, and even, on occasion, nonsense comedy. He gave
full treatment to the antiheroic, unromantic protagonist as the principal figure for use in heroic poetry. He dealt vividly with sexuality.
He made new uses of the traditional American and English interest
in foreign literatures and in translation. He developed a violently
antimechanical, experimental prosody. He emphasized precision, even
when the rules by which accuracy is judged might be unclear. He
used dramatic episodes rather than lyrical explanations as the structural basis of poetry, and so eliminated nearly all connective material.
Finally, he gave free rein to the fantastic, the nightmarish, and the
phantasmagoric. Not separately, in a succession of poems, but at once,
in one long poem, *The Waste Land,* Eliot synthesized these elements.
Without his dissolution of worn-out, contemporary traditions and his
creation of a tradition anew, as Frank Kermode has recently said,
"poetry had no future we can now seriously conceive of." Eliot gave
poetry back, not to the academies, but to the uses of civilization.

III

On each of these features of the poem, of course, a great deal
might be written. Here I can indicate only briefly the lines along
which more refined inquiry might proceed. Curiously, although writ-

ers who deal with Eliot as a person speak uniformly of his wit and good humor, literary critics have treated him with dead seriousness—perhaps in compensation for earlier attacks upon the poem as a hoax. In some ways it *is* a hoax, in that Eliot treats the most serious issues in comic ways: he is flippant in the face of the ghastly, offhand concerning "The Horror!" while yet (most apparently in his "Notes") seriously deadpan about trivia. He unhesitatingly and outrageously mixes his metaphors, fuses the grand with the prosaic, the material with the spiritual, the sentimental with the sexual, mirth with anguish. This is high comedy, in the extravagant traditions of Chaucer, the American tall tale, *Candide, Don Quixote*. The poem is a hoax—Allen Tate has said that Eliot's humor is "unmistakably American"—in the same way that Huckleberry Finn's book is a hoax: if it leads us to the heart of darkness, it also gives us the wit by and through which to endure our journey. In a very useful essay, Elizabeth Sewell has written of Eliot as a nonsense poet. Certainly, within an elaborately controlled, logical framework, he did at times follow Émile Cammaerts's proposals in *The Poetry of Nonsense* by surrendering his verse to the random flow of verbal associations, and achieving a language of great diversity, free, above all, from the empty seriousness of much late Victorian verse. "In *The Waste Land*," Eliot told an interviewer in 1959, "I wasn't even bothering whether I understood what I was saying." In 1922 he needed to take the risk of writing nonsense in order to write at all. Good readers—Pound first of all—would see the sense in the nonsense. Perhaps this aspect of Eliot's wit is best characterized by Robert Frost's general description of style in poetry: "Style is the way the man takes himself; and to be at all charming or even bearable, the way is almost rigidly prescribed. If it is with outer seriousness, it must be with inner humor. If it is with outer humor it must be with inner seriousness."

Eliot was at first accused of constructing his poem from pieces of translated material. Wars in modern times, it is true, have always been followed by a revival of interest in past and foreign literatures; but to this interest Eliot gives a series of brilliant twists. Not only does he often translate with great originality, he also insists, by his very unwillingness to translate fully,[5] that translation must not open an escape into the past, but an entry into the present. It must lead into, not away from. Particularly in the final lines of the poem, what might otherwise have been a retreat suggests, rather, a pushing off into new waters, a going forward—as William Carlos Williams put it

[5] Baudelaire's lines: "Fourmillante cité, cité pleine de rêves,/Où le spectre en plein jour raccroche le passant" become simply "Unreal City" for Eliot.

in *Paterson:* "a reply to Latin and Greek with the bare hands; a
gathering up; a celebration."

Corresponding to Eliot's new subject matter and point of view was
his prosody, one which he invented to convey musically the flux and
confusion, the harshness and sharpness, the fusing of the original and
the traditional—above all, the variability—which he found at the
heart of the world he depicted. In "The Music of Poetry" Eliot
writes: "I know that a poem, or a passage of a poem, may tend to
realize itself first as a particular rhythm before it reaches expression
in words, and that a rhythm may bring to birth the idea and the
image." He allows his language primarily to create his music, but
gives his prosody, too, freedom enough to be creative. In short, Eliot's
prosody is fundamentally opposed to the mechanically regular im-
position of traditional rhythms, stresses, or tempos upon an idea;
rather, he proceeds intuitively to innovate out of familiar patterns.
He had learned from Pound how to modify conventional prosody by
use of the rhythms of ordinary speech; he also keeps his prosody intelligible and interesting by fastening upon patterns of speech which
are suggestively familiar. He makes his own conventions, and teaches
the reader to accept them, through a brilliant use of syntactical parallels, through reiterating words and grammatical constructions, through
making his rhythmic interruptions and juxtapositions accurate ana-
logues to the poem's themes. W. K. Wimsatt and Monroe C. Beardsley,
calling Eliot "a wise and shifty modern poet, always in search of
rhythmical invention," contend that he moves freely and subtly in
and out of, and often coalesces, strong-stress and syllable-stress meters
even in single stanzas.[6] "This," they conclude, "is something remarkable in the history of metrics." Eliot made, in short, a cogent and
intelligible prosody by using violent irregularities of rhythm, tempo,
and intonation to dramatize a world no longer felt to be regular.
At the same time he gave his experiments in prosody intelligibility
by freshly reworking techniques traditional in English verse.

That Eliot would some years later turn almost exclusively to play-
writing reminds one of the extent to which his criticism between
1917 and 1925 was concerned with questions of the drama and suggests that *The Waste Land* may be looked to for elements of drama.

6 They define "strong-stress" in verse as "meter . . . with [an] indeterminate or
relatively indeterminate number of syllables between the stresses"; and "the other
meter, of the great English tradition (Chaucer to Tennyson), which is a syllable-
stress meter, that is, a meter of counted syllables and of both major and minor
stresses." ("The Concept of Meter: An Exercise in Abstraction," *PMLA*, LXXIV
[1959], 592.)

As early as 1931 Edmund Wilson, writing of "the essentially dramatic character of [Eliot's] imagination," concluded that *The Waste Land* "especially . . . owes a large part of its power to its dramatic quality." The poem is marked with effective shifts in tone and imagery, striking juxtapositions in theme and situation, and an extraordinary interchange of fleeting characters. It vibrates both with the striking drama of outward contrasts and the inward Jamesian drama of the mind interacting with multifarious aspects of the mind of Europe. Ultimately, of course, Eliot's essential drama is that of the mind, with intense awareness, coming upon itself.

Unquestionably, Eliot draws in *The Waste Land* upon recollections of an actual London, and in large part accurately provides a literal geography for his poem. But it is the geography of mind and imagination in which he is really interested, and that scene, obviously, has become fantastic and nightmarish, grotesque and surreal—a genuine "dream-dump" of the imagination, as Nathanael West later said. Browning had earlier depicted such a world in "Childe Roland to the Dark Tower Came," a poem to which Eliot appropriately turns in the concluding lines of his own poem since his subject, like Browning's, is the dream of terror in modern life, for which the modern city is an appropriate symbol. Eliot subsumed city life into poetry, as no American since Whitman had done, by concentrating upon its nightmarish, but also its marvelous, qualities; he saw it both as an illusion, deeply deceptive, and as a mirage, enticing and appealing. It provided phantoms of horror together with phantoms of delight; the prospects of the decay of man and the possibilities for his renewal. In short, the city—which the sociologist Frank Parsons called "the aggregation of all that is best in civilization and all that is worst in the remnants of barbarism"—was, as a symbol, a richly ambiguous repository of meaning. Eliot depicted both possibilities, simultaneously, and created the Unreal City which could offer at once terror and delight.

In his *Essay on Rime* (1945) Karl Shapiro asks:

> And who will parse the broken measure of
> *The Waste Land,* our world-weary masterpiece
> In which the very metric tells the tale?
> Who will devise the necessary scale
> To read this rhyme as Milton's has been read?

Shapiro's question is for this collection of criticisms, and for the readers who learn from them, to answer. The disagreement evidenced in these pages is the best suggestion possible of the extent to which

The Waste Land sensitively reflects the modern and also the eternal human condition. Eliot's memorial tribute to Yeats—"He is one of those few whose history is the history of their own time, who are a part of the consciousness of the age which cannot be understood without them"—is equally true of himself and, in particular, of *The Waste Land*. The very history of the criticism of this poem is a characteristic aspect of the history of our time, its conflicts, needs, and indecisions; and insofar as we can respond freshly to the poem, even insofar as we can read its critics understandingly, we explore a vital part of modern experience.

Eliot was to write in "The Three Voices of Poetry" that, "when the words are finally arranged in the right way . . . [the poet] can say to the poem: 'Go away! Find a place for yourself in a book—and don't expect *me* to take any further interest in you.' " After the poet's dismissal of the poem, after it has found its place in a book and in the history of the language, after the critics have had their say and the nature and the background of the poem have been described, the poem remains. To it the reader can, and must, still go.

PART ONE

Interpretations

The Waste Land and the Modern World

John Crowe Ransom

Twice only have I written pieces about Eliot, and now I have to make two recantations. The first time I scolded him for *The Waste Land,* with what I took to be its academic trick of recondite allusions on the one hand, and on the other hand its want of a firm and consistent prosody, such as I seemed to require. I was mistaken about the allusions. It turned out quickly, and increasingly, that they meant a great deal to the members of a very important public. These were the remarkably bright young scholars and critics who aspired in that age to a complete learning, including the precise identification of original texts which might be referred to, even if ever so slightly. They were as tough-minded as they were competent, and when they succeeded they were elated like professional sportsmen over their triumphs. But they were most challenged when Eliot gave them sly literary allusions from which some religious or moral faith depended, and over which hovered the sense of a secret passage from Eliot's mind to theirs. Eliot was always a religious poet, though he never propounded the dogmas of his faith, which evidently was rather eclectic; it could be Hebraic, or Christian, or Greek, or even Oriental. But those sturdy people who studied his *Waste Land* felt the passion which he had put into the transaction. They must have had a feeling of having been starved of something or other in the poverty of their intellectual interests, and now of knowing that what they had missed was the religious sense in which they had been reared. (I am afraid it becomes less and less in the rearing of our successive modern generations.) Their vague uneasiness in their occupation became a good plain nostalgia when they saw what it had meant. Eliot gave back their old world to them. It was a beautiful predicament, and repeated many times.

From "Gerontion," by John Crowe Ransom. Sewanee Review, *LXXIV (Spring 1966), 389–90. Copyright © 1966 by the University of the South. Reprinted by permission of the* Sewanee Review.

Stephen Spender

Today one can feel envious of a poet who is attacked by adversaries whose function seems to be to define only their own incomprehension, making themselves the foil to his intelligence. Their mistake was to think that the intellect is necessarily cold. If Eliot had been cold we would not have been drawn to him. The fact is, of course, that his intellect burned white-hot. What attracted the young poets to *The Waste Land* was that rhythmically the language was so exciting. To say this is to say a great deal, for rhythmic excitement of the order of *The Waste Land* is rare in poetry, and not necessary to it. What is necessary is that rhythm should be interesting, unique to the poet, the handwriting of his sensibility, even of something beyond sensibility, the indefinable quality of his being. All Eliot's poetry has uniqueness and interest, but *The Waste Land* does more than hold the reader's interest and admiration, it makes the poetry become a passion to the reader. When this happens with a poet, his readers take up an entirely new attitude to him. Of modern poets, one could see it happen to Yeats when he published *The Tower,* which has rhythmic excitement. Although what is now perhaps Yeats's most famous poem, "The Second Coming," was written as early as 1922, it was not until *The Tower* that readers really woke up to the fact that Yeats had emerged completely from the Celtic Twilight, and from being a minor had become a major poet of the present century.

One learned from *The Sacred Wood* of Eliot's views about tradition. But I myself enjoyed reading *The Sacred Wood* as I might any excellent critical essay, relishing particularly the quotations from the Elizabethans. It was not *The Sacred Wood* so much as the rhythmic excitement of *The Waste Land* and *The Tower* which really gave me an appetite to look for the same excitement in past poetry. . . .

Apart from *The Waste Land,* Eliot's only poem which has this quality is "Gerontion," which after *The Waste Land* is his poem the most Elizabethan in feeling. One might say that intellect in Eliot is Dantesque, but up to the *Four Quartets,* the passion is Elizabethan.

From "Remembering Eliot," by Stephen Spender. Sewanee Review, *LXXIV (Winter 1966), 66–67. Copyright © 1966 by the University of the South. Reprinted by permission of the* Sewanee Review.

Steven Foster

Like the Relativity Theory's conception of the universe, *The Waste Land* is a mathematical and symbolic scheme of forces, pressures, tensions, oscillations, and waves. It does not adhere to any classical structure by the character of its rhythms, stanzaic pattern, vocabulary, or general style. Essentially a poem extolling flux and discontinuity and an impressive variety that recedes into the obscure and inchoate, its symbols are neither regular nor precise; its allusions echo and re-echo with changed voices; it treats time and distance contemptuously, as if they were random accidents; it is obsessed with events rather than persons. One hardly need say that it is, in a much larger sense than "Hugh Selwyn Mauberly" two years before, a theoretical experiment in structures.

In the Red Queen's country Alice had to run as fast as possible to remain in the same place. Tiresias seems to have a similar role; at least while everything ages, his own existence persists like Rip Van Winkle's. In 1911 Einstein demonstrated that such a phenomenon was possible when an organism approximated the speed of light. If this constant were exceeded Bradley's fantasy of backward-running time would result:

> There was a young girl named Miss Bright,
> Who could travel much faster than light.
> She departed one day,
> In a Relative way,
> And came back on the previous night. (Anon.)

Poor Sibyl in her cage might instead have become younger each year. This is not to say that Tiresias' peculiarly timeless existence is directly related to particles in a cyclotron, but to suggest the possibilities which arise from a juxtaposition of *The Waste Land* and relativity.

"In the new theory we are concerned with *events* both temporal and spatial at once, not with bodies." [1] Eliot's poem properly consists of events and the arbitrary intervals between them. The term "interval" is not exact; "variable relation" might be more precise. The

From "Relativity and The Waste Land: *A Postulate," by Steven Foster.* Texas Studies in Literature and Language, *VII (Spring 1965), 86–88. Copyright © 1965 by University of Texas Press. Reprinted by permission of the publisher.*
[1] Bertrand Russell, *The ABC of Relativity* (London: Kegan Paul, Trench, Trubner & Co., Ltd., 1925), p. 69.

events themselves have no significance beyond the poet's subjective treatment of them; the "variable relations" between events are subject to simple or inexplicable caprice. Events can be mythical (the Hanged God and the others of *The Golden Bough*), anthropological (the Fisher King, the various situations of the Tarot pack), historical (Elizabeth, Magnus Martyr, Carthage, Athens, etc.), literary (*ad infinitum*), or part of the "specious present," and each allusion has an amorphous space-time existence. The aggregate of these "point-events" [2] is the poem's world, the solely mental world of poetic consciousness. Within this scheme events are either *literally transposed* upon each other with little or no "interval" (e.g., "But at my back from time to time I hear . . ."), or *partially divorced* so that elements are in a more or less successive order, as in the Tiresias passage, or in

> Unreal City
> Under the brown fog of a winter noon
> Mr. Eugenides, the Smyrna merchant . . . ,

where each line represents a different event. The rules are not firm; there are extremes, modifications, and exceptions. Basically what is demonstrated is a mind working with a *personal* history in a relativistic manner.

To enlarge upon the importance of this technique, the poem expresses at least one of Wyndham Lewis' so-called "time-cult" characteristics: "a metaphysical conviction that subjective experience [of time] alone can be possible or valid." [3] This nonmeasurable Einsteinian "I-time" signifies a new stylistic approach which is disconcerting but which informs the poem throughout. "To clap on your felt, and, simply by wishing that you were Anywhere, straightway to be There! Next to clap on your other felt, and, simply by wishing that you were Anywhen, and straightway to be Then!" [4] This instantaneous teleportation between disparate events, as said before, results from an arbitrary treatment of time and space by an individual exertion of free will which denies causative laws. Because they are "variable quantities," time, distance, even weight, differ from one observer

[2] A phrase of Sir Arthur Eddington, *Space, Time, and Gravitation: An Outline of the General Relativity Theory* (New York: Harper & Row, Publishers, 1959), p. 186.

[3] *Rolf Fjelde*, "Time, Space, and Wyndam Lewis," *Western Review*, XV: 3 (1951), 209.

[4] Thomas Carlyle, *Sartor Resartus*, quoted in Bowyer and Brooks, eds., *The Victorian Age* (New York: Appleton-Century-Crofts, 1954), pp. 172–173.

to the next, and it is at least theoretically possible, according to Russell, "for the time interval between two events to be zero: when the one event is the seeing of the other." [5] In *The Waste Land* the implications are plain enough throughout its form. For example, in the first thirty lines of "The Fire Sermon," where the collection of historical elements is quite concentrated, Eliot handles this past arbitrarily, subjectively. Spenser's "Prothalamion," Psalm 137, Marvell's "Coy Mistress," Ezekial's "dry bones," the Fisher King, *The Tempest,* Day's "Parliament of Bees," a ballad from Australia, Sweeney, footwashing ritual, and Verlaine's "Parsifal" all contribute their part to the poetic scene. They are brought into such proximity that the time-lapse between them often gives the illusion of being zero; "one event is the seeing of the other." Notice that time has not been arrested in the simple but inadequate worldwide knife-edged "now" of Newtonian imagery. The poet manipulates these elements as if they existed within a spatial-temporal continuum, each containing its own private duration, each snatched as a selective cross section from the flux. Altogether, these lines constitute a funny little world of rivers, rat's feet, and soda water that has a certain awkward continuity and a sense of timelessness. Because the fragments, literary or otherwise, are purely relative, they are depicted in an arbitrary, not-a-bit-impossible relationship by a poet who cannot demand that they take fixed positions in a "clock-work" history because, relativity permitting, they never quite have.

A viable examination of what *The Waste Land* could very well be saying must begin with its tone of voice and a denial of the usual attitude that the poet is nostalgic and disillusioned, detesting the weary present as he remembers the noble past. The shifting cadences do not grind out the broken music of disillusionment, longing, terror, horror, or what have you that is the literary halo effect of the "Lost Generation." . . . The tone is rather clinical, astringent, skeptical, intellectual. What little emotion there is radiates from the irony which makes the poem work. The poem succeeds so beautifully where the *Cantos* fail precisely because emotion is absent and the poet never need fear being out of character; like a calculus, its designer never intrudes upon his material.

---

[5] Russell, *op. cit.,* p. 55.

Herbert Howarth

[Eliot] wrote at a time when two technical suggestions had come to his notice. Whether he took them up consciously, or whether the impression they had made on him on the eve of illness determined their use without any conscious scrutiny and decision on his part, they appear to have contributed to the method of his poem. One derived from *Le Sacre du Printemps;* the other came from Pound.

In the summer of 1921 Eliot saw *Le Sacre du Printemps* in London, was involved in the warfare over it that almost separated friends, watched Diaghilev surrender to the Philistines and withdraw it after three performances, and defended and interpreted it in his "London Letter" to the *Dial.* Its music, he told the *Dial,* metamorphosed the "rhythm of the steppes" into "the scream of the motor horn, the rattle of machinery, the grind of wheels, the beating of iron and steel, the roar of the underground railway, and the other barbaric cries of modern life." It brought home the continuity of the human predicament: primitive man on the dolorous steppes, modern man in the city with its "despairing noises"; the mind of the one a continuation of the mind of the other, the essential problem unchanging. Eliot's interpretation of Stravinsky suggests that a theme of *The Waste Land* is the unchanging predicament of man, and the unchanging remedy; and that Eliot realized that the theme required the capture of the frightening barbaric sounds, and (since poetry combines music and pictures) of the frightening or poignant images of man's environment; and that he equally realized that if he could capture these effects he would create the contemporary literature which no writer in English had yet created: he would bring a literature which had not yet had a Stravinsky, and lagged behind, level with European music. In another *Dial* letter, written two months earlier, he wrote a sentence which throws further light on the method: he pointed out that contemporary, as contrasted with earlier, ballet was at once more sophisticated and more simplified; and "what is needed of art is a simplification of current life into something rich and strange." The

From Notes on Some Figures Behind T. S. Eliot, *by Herbert Howarth. (Boston: Houghton Mifflin Company, 1964), pp. 234–37. Copyright © 1964 by Houghton Mifflin Company and Chatto and Windus Ltd. Reprinted by permission of the author and publishers.*

last words echo *The Tempest,* the alchemical drama which *The Waste Land* echoes. In *The Waste Land* Eliot worked by bold, simplifying strokes to metamorphose the despairing sounds, the desperate sights, of his world into the rich and strange. . . .

In the *Dial* of January 1921 Pound commented on Cocteau's *Poésies 1917–1920.* He claimed that Cocteau, inheriting from the *école de Laforgue,* wrote the poetry of the city intellect, a poetry which reflected the intersecting pluralities of the city:

> The life of a village is narrative; you have not been there three weeks before you know that in the revolution et cetera, and when M. le Comte et cetera, and so forth. In a city the visual impressions succeed each other, overlap, overcross, they are "cinematographic." . . .

In Eliot's city poem the visual impressions "succeed each other, overlap, overcross. . . ." As the original draft of *The Waste Land* on which Pound performed his Caesarian operation—that is, did the "cutting"—has disappeared, we cannot know to what extent the "cinematographic" technique was already in play in Eliot's version, to what extent it was imposed by Pound at the final stage. My supposition is that the original already brought the technique to bear, not because Eliot was interested in cinema (for he seems to have been resistant to it as an art form until the late date when he sanctioned, and participated in, the preparation of *Murder in the Cathedral* for the screen) but because, with the help of Pound's sentence in the *Dial,* he perceived that the technique was right for communicating the rhythm of London where the eye passes moment by moment from green to drab, from grim to nostalgic; and that Pound, when he saw the draft, approved, only thought that Eliot had not pushed the process far enough: Pound had perceived the essentials of cinema, and cut with ruthlessness and taste to complete the poem's cinematographic form.

Morris Freedman

"Eliot," remarked Edmund Wilson, "fears vulgarity . . . at the same time that he is fascinated by it." One of the signs of Eliot's

Morris Freedman, "Jazz Rhythms and T. S. Eliot," South Atlantic Quarterly, LI (1952), 423, 425, 427. Copyright © 1952 by Duke University Press. Reprinted by permission of the South Atlantic Quarterly.

fascination is his attempt to capture the rhythm and quality of speech on the vulgate level and use them for poetry. Eliot has, of course, generally brought into poetry the idiom of conversation, but in most places it is a conversation that comes from the mouths and appeals to the ears of persons on his cultural level. Often, however, as part of his general consciousness and general theme of the contrasts within our civilization, he has introduced echoes of popular jazz songs both as quotations and, more interestingly, in attempts to reproduce colloquial dialogue. Eliot's experiments with jazz rhythms are of particular interest in helping us understand one direction of his poetry and also in briefly posing the question of a contemporary drama in verse.

Jazz rhythms in poetry are a recent manifestation, since jazz music itself, from which they are derived, is not more than a half-century old. No system for the analysis of jazz rhythms exists, but an examination of Eliot's use of such rhythms both in fragments and in whole poems, together with references to the attempts of others in this direction, will reveal some of the principles of jazz rhythms. . . .

The Waste Land, in which Eliot juxtaposes pictures of the present world against the past, has a number of unmistakable jazz rhythms, particularly those that are fragments of popular songs, and several lines that have a jazz flavor. . . .

What Eliot seems to have intended with his jazz rhythms . . . is something like the occasional introduction into classical symphonic music of the dissonantal blare of the derby-covered trumpet. Strauss, for example, uses jazzlike overtones in occasional themes in the midst of otherwise more or less traditional music to convey particular meanings. The jazz rhythms serve their purpose remarkably well, for they jar us into attention and make the poetry a constantly alive thing, requiring from the reader an unusual concentration to get not only the dictionary meaning of the words but also their musical significance. At the same time, since Eliot deals with widely known rhythms (children, as has been shown, use jazz rhythms), everyone in a sense gets something from these poems. Even the nonintellectual, even, possibly, the illiterate, hearing about Mrs. Porter and her daughter who wash their feet in soda water against the background of the gracefulness of Spenser, say, or Eliot himself, must realize that something is going on.

Roy Harvey Pearce

The Waste Land has become such an assured part of the twentieth century consciousness, one of the major vehicles for its sensibility, that we easily forget the transformation it worked. Realizing some of the possibility latent in "Gerontion," it in effect at once proposed and confirmed a new basic style so powerful that the older basic style, charged deeply with egocentrism, would no longer be viable unless it met the challenge Eliot put to it.

The disparate materials of which The Waste Land is composed are designed to lose their disparateness in the composing. Tiresias, the Fisher King, Phlebas, the Thames maidens, and the rest—each participates in the life of the other, and so contributes to the single-minded effect of the poem: not because of what he is but because of what he manifests, negatively or positively, for good or for bad. Even the reader is made out to be one of the poem's personae. The Waste Land, insofar as it succeeds in its intention, offers us everything—locales, personae, motifs, structure—everything but a poet assured in his ability to make a poem. Certainly the poet is there, as his wit, intelligence, and imagination are there. But he can pretend not to be, except as he is but one bootless protagonist among many such. This, in any case, is a principal attribute of his particular kind of make-believe: that the poet is there only so that he may compose a poem which, in the light of his ultimate vision, will make his existence unnecessary.

He makes Tiresias, his principal protagonist, into a shape-shifter, unstable, uncertain of the powers of his own sense and sensibility, his creativity lying in his wise passiveness. Tiresias is not at the center of the history which the poem epitomizes; he does not have the power to be at the center of anything. Nor is the effect that of Eliot's giving him such a power. Rather, Eliot's studies and his meditations appear to have taught him that such a protagonist must have existed at various times, his intelligence and his power for action determined by the situation in which he was placed. So it is with all the other materials—fragments of folklore, belles-lettres, myth, cultural history, and the like—which fill out the poem. The poet's genius is in so in-

Roy Harvey Pearce, "Eliot: The Poetics of Myth," The Continuity of American Poetry (Princeton, N. J.: Princeton University Press, 1961), pp. 306–9. Copyright © 1961, by Princeton University Press. Reprinted by permission of the publisher.

sistently seeming to have none. Even his "modern" Tiresias, who opens the poem, is not endowed with the ability to "do" anything. The poem, taken as a pronouncement on the nature of man, argues against the possibility of what I have called, in reference to Emily Dickinson, authentic autobiography. For such a possibility would inevitably argue the significance of the existence of the poet as a radically free self. The development of *The Waste Land* is such as theoretically to do away with that self, actually to put it in its place, low in the scale of things. The poet ostentatiously removes himself from his poem. Such ostentation derives from his actual creative role, to be sure; still, it is such as to urge that we minimize his relevance to his creation.

Eliot's method in *The Waste Land* is constantly to define the persons in the poem in terms of that which they are not. They cannot even directly conceive of that which they are not; they do not have the power to set going within themselves that process of action and reaction whereby they may begin to establish their own identity. They are denied even that last resort of the self-reliant, suicide. *The Waste Land*, thus, cannot be self-contained. For if it were, it would *a fortiori* argue for the possibility that somehow one or another of its protagonists might in and of himself do or make something. That enormous range of allusiveness which has set so many exegetes to work is accordingly the central technique of the poem, as it is the means of preventing the self-containment which any single poem, written by any single man, might achieve merely by virtue of its singleness. This, of course, is the major technique of the *Cantos,* too, but with this difference: that Pound will so control the allusive quality of his poem that it will be sufficient unto itself and will thereby manifest the power of him who has made it so; hence the poet will set himself up, epically, as a hero whose condition of life is one toward which, in reading the poem, his reader may aspire.

In *The Waste Land* Eliot sees more clearly than Pound ever has the direction in which a poet of his commitments must move. For example, there is the exquisitely contrived *mélange* of allusions at the end of "The Burial of the Dead"—

". . . Stetson!
"You who were with me in the ships at Mylae!
"That corpse you planted last year in your garden,
"Has it begun to sprout? Will it bloom this year?
"Or has the sudden frost disturbed its bed?
"Oh keep the Dog far hence, that's friend to men,

"Or with his nails he'll dig it up again!
"You! hypocrite lecteur!—mon semblable,—mon frère!"

The protagonist's friend Stetson, met on a London street, is identified as one who fought at the Battle of Mylae. This battle must be a mythic analogue to Jutland, surely; but the reference is to the battle at which Carthage was defeated and so serves to put the immediate fact of Jutland into deeper perspective. Then, as though the poet were trying to report the result of the battle, there is a corpse, treated half-graphically as buried in a vegetation ritual: so that the fact of death is not treated directly, but in the context of a ceremony which begins to make it meaningful. Then there is the twisted quotation from Webster, which, because of its source and provenience, at once marks the botching of a ritual and draws our attention to the poet's role as recorder, not creator. Then, if the reader, drawing a deep breath, has perhaps begun to sense how the carefully wrought consolidation of allusions does indeed argue for the creative presence of the poet, the last line transforms this argument into one for rather the creative presence of the reader. Yet, even this is managed indirectly, through an allusion to Baudelaire; so that the reader is not allowed to keep that private identity deriving from his sense of being "involved" in the poem. Or rather, such private identity as the reader has is made out to be a product of his discovering something whose power, import, and significance derive from a source other than himself.

Strictly speaking, there is no individual action which can be *imitated* in this mythic poem. There is potentially a communal action, a ritual, but it is as yet one which can only be observed. Eliot is still the poet as philosophical anthropologist. The poems of the participative ritual were to come later. *The Waste Land* made their coming inevitable. Interpreting the history of culture as a history of ritual forms, it postulated the existence of that single transcendent ritual in which alone the person would discover the power whereby he might move and act and be.

Such ritual, not directly participated in because considered as an historical-cultural rather than a theological fact, becomes explicitly the technique of *The Waste Land* in the final part of the concluding section, "What the Thunder Said." There are the ritual words, listened to from afar and registered in a "dead" language: *Datta, Dayadhvam, Damyata—Give, Sympathize, Control.* (True enough, these words are proved not *really* to be dead, for they have much to signify for us. The point, however, is that Eliot cannot find the

properly ritualistic words in the language of any culture presently
"alive.") *Make,* much less *Create,* is not part of the poet's vocabulary.
He has only the fragments which he has shored against his ruins, the
materials out of a world now known to be mythic, transhistorical.
Eliot comments thus on these last lines in his Notes: "Cf. . . . F. H.
Bradley, *Appearance and Reality,* p. 346. 'My external sensations are
no less private to myself than are my thoughts or my feelings. In
either case my experience falls within my own circle, a circle closed
on the outside; and, with all its elements alike, every sphere is opaque
to the others which surround it. . . . In brief, regarded as an existence which appears in a soul, the whole world for each is peculiar
and private to that soul.' "

It has been customary to ascribe much of Eliot's concern for the
limitation, isolation, and untrustworthiness of the self—the simple,
separate person—to his reading of Bradley. This may well be so. But
there is a larger dimension in which Eliot's poetry must be placed,
that of the continuity of American poetry against which he so mag-
nificently set himself and which, by virtue of doing so, he forever
changed. The private world of the Adamic poet was a closed circle
too; but it was said to include within itself all possible worlds. That
possibility, it was believed, had simply to be brought to fruition by
the creative act. But for the mythic poet, man's private world was so
narrow and constrained that it had to be transcended. The power to
such transcendence could not possibly reside within man—nor, as it
develops in Eliot's later poetry, within history.

Interpretations of Individual Sections

I. The Burial of the Dead

John B. Vickery

Two phrases in T. S. Eliot's *The Waste Land,* both from "The Burial of the Dead" section, recall passages in Freud's *Totem and Taboo (The Basic Writings of Sigmund Freud,* ed. A. A. Brill, New York: 1938).

First, April is said to be mixing "memory and desire." The passage in Freud echoed by this phrase occurs in the chapter on "Taboo and the Ambivalence of Emotions." There Freud declares: "the dangerous magic power of the *mana* corresponds to two real faculties, the capacity of reminding man of his forbidden wishes, and the apparently more important one of tempting him to violate the prohibition in the service of these wishes. Both functions reunite into one, however, if we assume it to be in accord with a primitive psychic life that with the awakening of a memory of a forbidden action there should also be combined the awakening of the tendency to carry out the action. *Memory and temptation then again coincide.*" (*Totem and Taboo,* p. 833; stress is mine.)

Freud contends that the forbidden action which is remembered is nothing less than the slaying of the father by his sons who are jealous of his prerogatives (*Totem and Taboo,* pp. 915–16). This act, together with its attendant cannibalistic feast, ostensibly occurred during the primal state of society. With the development of society, according to Freud, the totem animal and then the god himself were substituted for the original father. The important point of all this is not that Eliot is providing a concealed Freudian account of the origin of religious consciousness. Rather the chief significance of this passage is that it suggests a clear reason for the ambivalent feelings in Eliot's

John B. Vickery, "Two Sources of 'The Burial of the Dead,'" Literature and Psychology, X *(Winter 1960), 3–4. Copyright © 1960 by* Literature and Psychology. *Reprinted by permission of the author and publisher.*

opening lines. It links mankind more closely to its god whose demise is mourned in this section of the poem. Humanity's desire for the god's rebirth is balanced by the memory of its share in his death.

Secondly, the phrase "Those are pearls that were his eyes," whose immediate source is, of course, *The Tempest,* is closely related to this same theme. In *Totem and Taboo* Freud says: "a process like the removal of the primal father by the band of brothers must have left ineradicable traces in the history of mankind and must have expressed itself the more frequently in substitutive formations the less it itself was to be remembered" (p. 925). And in a footnote, as an example of one such substitutive formation, he quotes Ariel's dirge for the death by water of Alonso, the same song on which Eliot has drawn. Seen in the context of *Totem and Taboo,* Eliot's line, whose metaphoric power critics have long recognized, achieves its full significance. It represents mankind's attempt to suppress its guilty involvement in the death of the god, the source of life, whose human equivalent is the father. And as the reiteration of this line in "A Game of Chess," the Fisher King passage in "The Fire Sermon," the Phoenician sailor of "Death by Water," and the Gethsemane scene in "What the Thunder Said" all attest, the poem as a whole, on one level at least, dramatizes man's slow, reluctant, and painful admission of his own guilt.[1]

William T. Moynihan

There is no distinction in *The Waste Land* between hell and contemporary life. The Hades through which Tiresias passes is a state of mind embracing various times and various lives in a present moment. It is the place of those "who lived without blame, and without praise," typified by the man "who from cowardice made the great refusal" (*Divine Comedy,* Canto III). The *Inferno* reference follows the expression "Unreal City." The only way in which London or any

[1] Objective evidences which tend to support this relationship are the facts that (1) *Totem and Taboo* first appeared in 1912 in periodical form in ample time for Eliot to see it before writing *The Waste Land;* (2) Eliot himself was in Germany, where presumably Freud's work would be readily accessible, just prior to the outbreak of World War I; (3) Eliot's own reviews of Webb's *Group Theories of Religion and the Religion of the Individual* and Wundt's *Elements of Folk Psychology,* in 1916 and 1917, respectively, reveal his interest in psychoanalysis and its connection with anthropology and comparative religion.

From "The Goal of the Waste Land Quest," by William T. Moynihan. From *Renascence, XIII: 1 (Autumn 1960), 175–76. Copyright © 1960 by William T. Moynihan. Reprinted by permission of the author and Renascence.*

other city is really *unreal* is in a system of thought where the "City of God" is contrasted with the "City of Man." As Blake says, "The cities man builds in this world express his desires to live an eternal civilized life in a New Jerusalem of which the Messiah is the cornerstone. . . ."

The important point in this final section of Part I that has been overlooked by critics is the nature of Eliot's satire there. The best commentary on this section is in the source of "hypocrite lecteur"— Baudelaire's introductory poem in *Les Fleurs du Mal*. Eliot's prime concern, like Baudelaire's, is with the ugly monster *Ennui*. Both see the contemporary scene in terms of a descent into hell caused, basically, by being neither hot nor cold. But they also see more. We have frequently been reminded of Eliot's debt to Webster and his acquaintance with fertility rites in connection with the lines: "Oh keep the Dog far hence, that's friend to men,/Or with his nails he'll dig it up again!" But these lines also echo Petronius' *Satyricon*. Given directions for the decoration of his monument at his grave, Trimalchio asks that "At the feet of my effigy you have my little bitch put . . ." —"bitch" here referring to his wife. Then, shortly after an argument with his wife, he cries, "All right! I'll make you long yet to dig me up again with your fingernails." The hell of Eliot's contemporary world thus lies between the poles of Baudelaire's *Ennui* and Petronius' decadence. We plant our corpses as Stetson of Mylae planted his Osiris effigy—aware of gentle April, aware simply of the turning of the wheel, aware of vegetation. "To plant a corpse" is Hollywood slang, the word "sprout" is humorous in a macabre sense, and as Eliot reads lines 74 and 75, his slow deliberate cadence picks up to the tempo of a punch line. The satire seems almost inescapable.

II. A Game of Chess

Bruce R. McElderry, Jr.

At line 128 of *The Waste Land* occurs an allusion which so far as I know has not been specifically annotated: [1] "O O O O that Shake-

From "Eliot's 'Shakespeherian Rag,'" by Bruce R. McElderry, Jr. American Quarterly, *IX (1957), 185–86. Copyright © 1957 by the* American Quarterly. *Reprinted by permission of the author and publisher.*

[1] In *The American Tradition in Literature* (eds., Sculley Bradley, Richard Croom Beatty, and E. Hudson Long), (New York: W. W. Norton & Co., 1956), II, 917, is an allusion to "a piece of ragtime music," but no details are given.

speherian Rag—/It's so elegant/So intelligent." This is a brief inter-
ruption in the first dialogue of "The Game of Chess," and to younger
readers must seem like a symbol of vulgarity fabricated by Eliot himself. Readers whose memories go back to 1912, however, may recall
"That Shakespearian Rag" as a hit tune of that year. The song is still
obtainable, and reference to its text gives Eliot's lines a sharper satirical thrust.

The song as a whole, with its "Bill Shakespeare," and such lines as
"Soon, 'As You Like It,' Brutus/We'll play a rag today," is utterly
tasteless. The chorus, which illustrates its tone, provided the source
for Eliot's lines.

> That Shakespearian rag,—
> Most intelligent, very elegant,
> That old classical drag,
> Has the proper stuff, the line "Lay on Macduff,"
> Desdemona was the colored pet,
> Romeo loved his Juliet—
> And they were some lovers, you can bet, and yet,
> I know if they were here today,
> They'd Grizzly Bear in a diff'rent way,
> And you'd hear old Hamlet say,
> "To be or not to be,"
> That Shakespearian Rag.[2]

As may be seen, Eliot has slightly altered the initial lines by adding the
O O O O and by introducing the syncopated—he—in "Shakespeherian."

No doubt the allusion to Shakespeare made this "rag" more effective in Eliot's context than "Everybody's Doin' It," "Ragging the Old
Vienna Roll," or "Be My Little Baby Bumble Bee"—some of the
lively competitors of "That Shakespearian Rag." But "That Shakespearian Rag" was also a genuine hit, and thus a proper symbol of
public taste at the period when Eliot was a graduate student at
Harvard. The publishers of the song listed it fourth among ten titles
in a *Variety* advertisement for July 19, 1912 (p. 25), adding this comment: "If you want a song that can be acted as well as sung send for
this big surprise hit." The song was featured again in advertisements
of September 6 (p. 34), October 25 (p. 27), November 22 (p. 27), and
December 20 (p. 80), twice as the first in the publisher's list. On

---

2 Copyright by Edward B. Marks Music Corporation, used by permission. The
song was originally published by Joseph W. Stern & Co. Gene Buck and Herman
Ruby wrote the lyric and Dave Stamper the music.

October 25 it was billed as "Roy Samuels' big hit in Ziegfield's Follies of 1912."

Though *Variety* fully confirms the vulgarity of 1912, there are some suggestions of the vitality of that remote era. W. C. Fields, Eddie Cantor, and the Marx Brothers were all young men, blatantly advertising their talents. The Six Brown Brothers were popularizing the saxophone. And Mae West was singing "Isn't She the Brazen Thing." Despite the low quality of "That Shakespearian Rag," the land was not wholly waste in 1912.

III. THE FIRE SERMON

Allen Tate

In *The Waste Land* the prestige of our secular faith gave to the style its special character. This faith was the hard, coherent medium through which the discredited forms of the historic cultures emerged only to be stifled; the poem is at once their vindication and the recognition of their defeat. They are defeated in fact, as a politician may be defeated by the popular vote, but their vindication consists in the critical irony that their subordinate position casts upon the modern world.

The typical scene is the seduction of the stenographer by the clerk, in "The Fire Sermon." Perhaps Mr. J. W. Krutch has not discussed this scene, but a whole generation of critics has, and from a viewpoint that Mr. Krutch has recently made popular: the seduction betrays the disillusion of the poet. The mechanical, brutal scene shows what love really is—that is to say, what it is scientifically, since science is truth: it is only an act of practical necessity, for procreation. The telling of the story by the Greek seer, Tiresias, who is chosen from a past of illusion and ignorance, permits the scene to become *a satire on the unscientific values of the past*. It was all pretense to think that love was anything but a biological necessity. The values of the past were pretty, absurd, and false; the scientific truth is both true and bitter. This is the familiar romantic dilemma, and the critics have read it into the scene from their own romantic despair.

There is no despair in the scene itself. The critics, who being in the state of mind I have described are necessarily blind to an effect of irony, have mistaken the symbols of an ironic contrast for the terms of a philosophic dilemma. It is the kind of metaphorical "logic" typical of romantic criticism since Walter Pater. Mr. Eliot knows too much about classical irony to be overwhelmed by a popular dogma in literary biology. For the seduction scene shows, not what man is, but what *for a moment* he thinks he is. In other words, the clerk stands for the secularization of the religious and qualitative values in the modern world. And the meaning of the contrast between Tiresias and the clerk is not disillusion, but irony. The scene is a masterpiece, perhaps the most profound vision that we have of modern man.

William M. Gibson

Though I do not suppose the fact has gone unobserved, to my knowledge no critic of *The Waste Land* has noted in print that the poet embedded a double Shakespearian sonnet in the section called "The Fire Sermon." The first of these sonnets begins with "The time is now propitious, as he guesses" (l. 236) and is almost perfectly regular; the second, which follows immediately, may be said to end with the couplet rhyme "mandoline/within" (ll. 261–62), and is irregular in several respects. It is with great skill and subtlety that Mr. Eliot has worked the perfect and the "decayed" sonnets into the rhythmic context of "The Fire Sermon." He leads up to the first through irregular blank verse marked by occasional rhymes, and he lets the second begin to crumble away from the sonnet pattern in the third quatrain by using only one rhyme ("Street" repeated) and by completing the sonnet with a line (262) that can just barely be read as iambic pentameter. The sonnets are partially concealed from the eye as well as from the ear. The first is set off in the typography only at its end, by a break or "white space" on the page; the second is broken by "white space" after its first two quatrains, the third quatrain and couplet running over into three concluding lines (263–265) without any mark of punctuation. Moreover, the turn of the first sonnet occurs at the third quatrain, which is spoken by Tiresias as observer in heightened language, and enclosed in parentheses; the final couplet,

William M. Gibson, "Sonnets in T. S. Eliot's The Waste Land," *American Literature, XXXII (1961), 465–66. Copyright © 1961 by Duke University Press. Reprinted by permission of the publisher.*

which should be climactic, flattens out strikingly with the false rhyme "kiss/unlit. . . ." The turn of the second, similarly, begins at the third quatrain and is initiated by a line from *The Tempest,* but is concluded only when the sonnet "runs over" into a seventeenth and final line.[1] Above all, these Elizabethan sonnets do not at first reading appear to be sonnets at all because their subject and manner are so little like the subject and manner of their models. The spiritless fornication of the "typist home at teatime" and the "young man carbuncular" scarcely bears love out "even to the edge of doom," as Shakespeare has it, and the "half-formed thought" of this far from lovely woman—"I'm glad it's over"—strikes a note very different from Spenser's, say, in the "Amoretti" or even from Shakespeare's "The expense of spirit in a waste of shame/is lust in action. . . ." The effect is parody and more than parody.

Recognizing that Mr. Eliot wrote this well-known passage in the form of a double sonnet does not alter its meaning essentially, for the meaning inheres in a dramatic action—the typist and the clerk violate the mystery of sexual union, with Tiresias, Goldsmith's foolish woman, and Prince Ferdinand as ghostly witnesses. But that meaning is measurably enhanced when the rhythms and rhymes of the Shakespearian sonnet echo in the mind, and when the mind perceives the ironic variations played upon the traditional form—a form prepared for of course by richly various references to Elizabethan literature and history earlier in the poem. The sonnet configuration creates, I suggest, certain expectations in the reader: an exalted view of love, a harmony of chiming quatrains, a fine turn of thought and feeling in the couplet. Mr. Eliot here disappoints and transmutes such expectations. He creates his own characteristic illuminations and composes his own harmony. He makes the sonnet form in this part of *The Waste Land* carry a fresh poetic burden, and thereby heightens a major theme of the entire work—the wrenching disparity between "lust in action" in the present, and love fulfilled or spiritual or tragic in the past.

[1] If the reader insists that the passage embodies a sonnet plus two further quatrains I should have to agree. But I should add that the presence of the first sonnet leads the reader to expect the quatrains will also turn into a sonnet—as roughly speaking, they do.

V. What the Thunder Said

D. C. Fowler

One of the most controversial passages in T. S. Eliot's *The Waste Land* occurs at the very end of the poem. It will be recalled that after the three statements of the thunder—Datta, Dayadhvam, Damyata— the poet concludes as follows:

> I sat upon the shore
> Fishing, with the arid plain behind me
> Shall I at least set my lands in order?
> London Bridge is falling down falling down falling down
> *Poi s'ascose nel foco che gli affina*
> *Quando fiam uti chelidon*—O swallow swallow
> *Le Prince d'Aquitaine à la tour abolie*
> These fragments I have shored against my ruins
> Why then Ile fit you. Hieronymo's mad againe.
> Datta. Dayadhvam. Damyata.
> Shantih   shantih   shantih

Reactions to this passage range all the way from E. M. Forster's skeptical query, "What does the scrap-heap of quotations at the end signify?" to Cleanth Brooks's favorable judgment, "The bundle of quotations with which the poem ends has a very definite relation to the general theme of the poem and to several of the major symbols used in the poem" (quoted from *T. S. Eliot: A Selected Critique,* ed. Leonard Unger [New York, 1948], pp. 13, 342). Interest in these concluding lines has been especially great since Mr. Eliot's conversion to Anglo-Catholicism. It has been alleged, on the one hand, that the poem exhibits no progression—that it ends where it began—and, on the other hand, that the poem contains promise of the subsequent conversion.

It is not my purpose to take up this debate over the state of Mr. Eliot's mind as exhibited in *The Waste Land.* Further, I find myself

From "The Waste Land: *Mr. Eliot's 'Fragments,'*" by *D. C. Fowler.* College English, *XIV (January 1953), 234–35.* Copyright © 1953 by the National Council of Teachers of English. *Reprinted with the permission of the National Council of Teachers of English and D. C. Fowler.*

in agreement with much of what has been said concerning the artistic propriety of the closing lines (e.g., cf. George Williamson, "The Structure of *The Waste Land*," *Modern Philology*, XLVII [1950], 196 f., 205 f.). I wish only to suggest here an obvious interpretation of the passage, on one level, which to my knowledge has not hitherto been proposed.

The protagonist, here identified with the Fisher King, sits on the shore fishing, with the arid plain behind him, and asks the question: "Shall I at least set my lands in order?" (cf. Isaiah 38:1). What follows is, it seems to me, on one level at least, nothing more than a charm, the purpose of which is to break the spell of the waste land. The foreign-language quotations provide the *abracadabra* element. Just as the hero of the Grail romances was expected to speak the proper words (usually in the form of a question) before the wounded king and his land could be restored, so the protagonist in *The Waste Land*, as both hero and king, utters an incantation designed to bring about the restoration of life in himself and his environment.

The potency of foreign or strange words in charms was considered to be great. Witness, for example, the use of Latin words and phrases in the Old English charms. The metrical charm *For Unfruitful Land* opens with an elaborate set of instructions (MS Cotton Caligula A. vii, British Museum; my own translation):

> Here is the remedy, how you might amend your acres, if they will not grow well, or where any wrongful thing is done by sorcery or witchcraft.
>
> Take then at night, ere it dawns, four turfs from four sides of the land and mark how they stood before. Take then oil and honey and yeast, and milk from all the cattle that are on that land, and part of each kind of . tree that grows on the land except hard wood, and part of every known herb except burdock alone, and put holy water thereon, and let it drip then thrice on the bottom of the turfs and then say these words:
>
> "*Crescite* wax, *et multiplicamini* and multiply, *et replete* and replenish, *terre* this earth. *In nomine patris et filii et spiritus sancti sit benedicti.*"

The charm continues with more detailed instructions and reaches its climax in the famous passage beginning with the invocation:

> Erce, Erce, Erce, mother of earth,
> May the Almighty grant, eternal Lord,
> Growing and flourishing acres . . .

and concludes with the instruction:

> Say then three times, *Crescite in nomine patris, sit benedicti. Amen* and *Pater noster* thrice.

Of course, the Old English charm *For Unfruitful Land* is quoted simply as an example. There can be no profit in searching for parallels in Mr. Eliot's text—such as the triple "Amen" compared with "Shantih shantih shantih"—since details in the charms vary widely. But it does seem to me that the "fragment" passage is best understood as a charm, and that the emotional impact of the poem is enhanced by such an interpretation.

If this explanation is accepted, what may we conclude about the progression of the poem? Is the protagonist saying "Avaunt!" to the horror of the waste land? My own opinion is that the end represents a definite advance over the negativism of the opening lines. But Mr. Eliot's fondness for irony precludes any hasty dogmatism.

"Notes" to *The Waste Land*

Hugh Kenner

In fact we shall do well to discard the notes as much as possible; they have bedevilled discussion for decades.

The writing of the notes was a last complication in the fractious history of the poem's composition; it is doubtful whether any other acknowledged masterpiece has been so heavily marked, with the author's consent, by forces outside his control. The notes got added to *The Waste Land* as a consequence of the technological fact that books are printed in multiples of thirty-two pages.

The poem, which had appeared without any annotation whatever in *The Criterion* and in the *Dial* (October and November 1922, respectively), was in book form too long for thirty-two pages of decent-sized print and a good deal too short for sixty-four. So Eliot (at length disinclined, fortunately, to insert *Gerontion* as a preface or to append the cancelled lyrics) set to work to expand a few notes in which he had identified the quotations, "with a view to spiking the guns of critics of my earlier poems who had accused me of plagiarism." [1] He dilated on the Tarot Pack, copied out nineteen lines from

From The Invisible Poet: T. S. Eliot, *by Hugh Kenner. (New York: Ivan Obolensky, Inc., 1959), pp. 150–52. Copyright © 1959 by Hugh Kenner. Reprinted by permission of the publisher.*

[1] This incredibly illiterate literary society seems to have been wholly unaware of the methods of Pope, or else to have supposed that a period allegedly devoted to "profuse strains of unpremeditated art" had rendered such methods obsolete.

Ovid and thirty-three words from Chapman's *Handbook of Birds of Eastern North America,* recorded his evaluation of the interior of the Church of St. Magnus Martyr, saluted the late Henry Clarke Warren as one of the great pioneers of Buddhist studies in the Occident, directed the reader's attention to a hallucination recorded on one of the Antarctic expeditions ("I forget which, but I think one of Shackleton's"), and eventually, with the aid of quotations from Froude, Bradley, and Hermann Hesse's *Blick ins Chaos,* succeeded in padding the thing out to a suitable length. The keying of these items to specific passages by the academic device of numbering lines—hence Eliot's pleasantry, twenty-four years later, about "bogus scholarship"—may be surmised to have been done in haste: early in *What the Thunder Said* a line was missed in the counting. "I have sometimes thought," Eliot has said, "of getting rid of these notes; but now they can never be unstuck. They have had almost greater popularity than the poem itself. . . . It was just, no doubt, that I should pay my tribute to the work of Miss Jessie Weston; but I regret having sent so many enquirers off on a wild goose chase after Tarot cards and the Holy Grail." We have license therefore to ignore them, and instead "endeavour to grasp what the poetry is aiming to be . . . to grasp its entelechy."

That the entelechy is graspable without source-hunting, and without even appeal to any but the most elementary knowledge of one or two myths and a few Shakespearean tags, is a statement requiring temerity to sustain in the face of all the scholarship that has been expended during a third of a century on these 434 lines. It inheres, however, in Dr. Leavis' admirably tactful account of the poem in *New Bearings,* and in Pound's still earlier testimony. In 1924 Pound rebutted a piece of reviewer's acrimony with the flat statement that the poem's obscurities were reducible to four Sanskrit words, three of which are

so implied in the surrounding text that one can pass them by . . . without losing the general tone or the main emotion of the passage. They are so obviously the words of some ritual or other.

One does need to be told that "shantih" means "peace."

For the rest, I saw the poem in typescript, and I did not see the notes till 6 or 8 months afterward; and they have not increased my enjoyment of the poem one atom. The poem seems to me an emotional unit. . . .

I have not read Miss Weston's *Ritual to Romance,* and do not at present intend to. As to the citations, I do not think it matters a damn which

is from Day, which from Milton, Middleton, Webster, or Augustine. I
mean so far as the functioning of the poem is concerned. One's incult
pleasure in reading *The Waste Land* would be the same if Webster had
written "Women Before Woman" and Marvell the *Metamorphoses*.

His parting shot deserves preservation:

This demand for clarity in every particular of a work, whether essential
or not, reminds me of the Pre-Raphaelite painter who was doing a twilight scene but rowed across the river in day time to see the shape of the
leaves on the further bank, which he then drew in with full detail.

Technique

Eric Thompson

Eliot has done a number of interesting things, I believe, to help us see the "plot" of *The Waste Land* while doing everything in his power to draw the "hypocrite lecteur" away from the "story." One such device is his use of tenses. Verb tenses are usually crucial in Eliot and in *The Waste Land* they are important stage signals as to the whereabouts of the action. The classic pattern in much great tragedy is illustrated by a formula to be found in Eliot's *Dry Salvages:* "And the way up is the way down, the way forward is the way back." In *The Waste Land,* as in *Oedipus Rex* and *Death of a Salesman* (to go from extreme to extreme) the protagonist is caught in a present that is in the grip of the past, and the past keeps erupting into the present demanding acknowledgment and acceptance of an entity that is always now. To investigate Eliot's verbs, strange as it may seem, is to investigate his action.

"The Burial of the Dead," Section I of *The Waste Land,* begins in the present tense: "April *is* the cruelest month," then almost immediately slides back into the past: "Winter *kept* us warm," "Summer *surprised* us." Yet (at the end of the first scene) the tenses glide upward toward an historical present: "I *read* much of the night" which then fuses with the ambiguous opening of Scene 2: "What *are* the roots that clutch?" which in turn becomes firmly grounded in the *now* of "Son of man, you *cannot* say, for you *know*," etc. The Hyacinth Garden episode that follows is firmly planted in an exact past time: "You *gave* me hyacinths first a year ago" (last April). And so is the visit to Madam Sosostris who "*had* a bad cold" (last winter). The "Unreal City" episode, time—dawn, season—winter, is past tense. "A crowd *flowed* over London Bridge," "I *had* not thought," "There I *saw* one I knew." But the concluding lines of the section make a violent entrance into the present time. "You! hypocrite lecteur!—

From "Appendix: The Waste Land," in T. S. Eliot: The Metaphysical Perspective, *by Eric Thompson. (Carbondale, Ill.: Southern Illinois University Press, 1963), pp. 146–48. Copyright © 1963 by Southern Illinois University Press. Reprinted by permission of the Southern Illinois University Press.*

mon semblable,—mon frère!" Cutting across these tenses—irrelevant
to the time sequence—but very relevant to the timeless core of the
action in Section I are three imperatives: "Come in under the shadow
of this red rock," "Fear death by water," and "Keep the dog far
hence." These commands make Eliot's stage bristle with action.

"The Game of Chess" (Section II), "The Fire Sermon" (Section
III), and "Death By Water" (Section IV) are for the most part fixed
in past time, except for the concluding lines in each section where
the grammar, as it were, forces us back into the present crisis: "Good
night, ladies," "O Lord thou pluckest/burning," and "Consider Phlebas." Section III (the puzzling "middle") has erratic tenses: "The
river's tent *is* broken" (despite the autumn setting) in contrast to "By
the waters of Leman I *sat* down and *wept*" in contrast to "But at my
back in a cold blast I hear" in contrast to "A rat *crept*" (winter). Mr.
Eugenides issues his invitation in a clearly marked past time—"*Asked*
me in demotic French*"—but the seduction of the typist is described in
present tense, perhaps because to be conscious with Teresias of action
is not to be in time.

Section IV is all past. "Phlebas . . . *Forgot*." But Section V erupts
into the present and the effect is as though after some delay there is
actual *action*. Eliot reinforces this impression by use of setting: it
must be Easter (April) and an April that is hot and dry (like summer), in a place that duplicates that at the beginning where Teresias
commands: "Come in under the shadow of this red rock." This locale
is the setting of the present crisis in the poem. In Section V, Eliot
holds a steady present tense straight through the first six stanzas—
with one exception, the fifth. This is the longest stretch of present
tense in the poem. It is as if, with notice of the death of Phlebas, the
Quester is born and we watch him move (at the end of the day) across
the desert plain at the base of the mountains, to arrive at night at the
Chapel Perilous. Then something peculiar occurs. The cock crows,
and the Thunder speaks, but the voice of God speaks in past tense.
This contrast, if we watch for it, is startling, and we are drawn to seek
explanations in order to realize, perhaps, that the way forward *is* the
way back, and that this judgment did occur in the past, but the
protagonist did not hear it. Now he does, and this is the important
breakthrough in his life. In short, the Thunder spoke, and man did
not hear it, though he lived what it spoke, and having lived it, now
re-utters the judgment to himself for himself.

The tenses in the coda are fascinating. We see the Fisher King
fishing in past tense (yet with the arid plain *behind* him), and we see
him using one of the few simple futures of the poem, "*Shall* I at least

set my lands in order?" (The others occur in "The Game of Chess.")
When the battery of fragments explodes, it is hard to tell where we
are. I am inclined to say we are in a past that is in the process of
being accepted and so is present.

George T. Wright

Probably on no other score has Eliot's work been so condemned as
for its choice and treatment of people. Yet the number of characters
who, directly or by immediately understood allusion, make their way
into his poems is phenomenal. Because of the peculiar allusive structure of his verse, it is difficult to draw a line between who is and
who is not actually *in* his poems. In one sense, only the old man, his
boy, and his housekeeper inhabit the world of "Gerontion"; in a
second sense, it is inhabited also by the Jew, Christ, Mr. Silvero,
Hakagawa, Madame de Tornquist, Fräulein von Kulp, De Bailhache,
Fresca, and Mrs. Cammel; in a third sense, it is inhabited by characters whom the old man's phrasing recalls—Vindici, Beatrice of *The
Changeling,* Everyman, Tennyson's Ulysses, Judas, and others, all of
whom are, when the allusions are perceived, hardly more shadowy
than the second-level characters or, indeed, than the boy, the housekeeper, or even the old man himself. In the same way *The Waste
Land* employs a small army of characters either present or recalled, all
of whom contribute to our impression of Eliot's treatment of people.
And other poems, especially those written no later than 1922, intro-
duce people almost as multitudinously as Hardy's *The Dynasts.*

But the peculiarity of number is not the only distinguishing mark
of Eliot's characters. Their kind of actuality is rather different from
that of any other poet's people. In the first place, the poet cares little
for their individual qualities; what he cares about is their relationship to certain enduring archetypal roles. They act, consequently, if
they act at all, in conformity to the demands of their roles rather
from what we should call personal motives. The details of their talk,
of their manners, of their gestures, are idiosyncratic rather of their
roles than of themselves. The shifting of the candles by Madame de
Tornquist, the entrance of Doris from the bath, the successive actions
of the typist and the clerk, all reflect nothing individual in these

George T. Wright, The Poet in the Poem *(Berkeley and Los Angeles: University
of California Press, 1960), pp. 60–63. Copyright © 1960 by the University of California Press. Reprinted by permission of the publisher.*

persons—no charming inconsistency, no personal diabolism—but are clearly ritual actions that they perform in order to fulfill their roles in a ritual drama.

It is this ritual aspect of his characters which makes them so different from the people we usually know. We are accustomed to thinking of people as individuals, or at least as types familiar to our culture, but, for the purposes of his poetry at least, Eliot gives us people whose archetypal roles characterize them more fully than do their cultural and individual peculiarities. Occasionally what we think of as a human face breaks through the archetypal mist—Prufrock, the Lady, sometimes even Sweeney, and the poet himself in *Four Quartets*. Such characters as these are exhibited in their culture in somewhat more detail; the poet permits them greater local definition. But they still retain their roles in the ritual drama, still speak and act in response to ritual demands. The typical character in Eliot's poetry is like the Lady at the beginning of "A Game of Chess," identified only by her room and the objects it contains, by her perfume and by the disembodied words she utters. We see everything in her setting but of her nothing but her hair. Naturally enough: *she* is not important; what is important is the role that she plays, a role defined more fully by her environment than by anything peculiar to herself.

At the same time, though, the contemporaneity of the archetypal is stressed. Most of Eliot's characters are drawn from modern European culture, and much of the point in their actions lies in the juxtapositions within them of contemporary and eternal human qualities. This arrangement enables Eliot to present the modern world as merely one of an infinite number of disguises that permanent human reality may wear. And just as individual qualities are slighted, so the culturally accidental fuses into the humanly essential.

Since Eliot's characters do not usually receive substantial individuality, and since even their cultural characteristics give way to their human ritual roles, they are often unstable. Different persons who play the same archetypal role tend to "melt" into one another, and even the different roles merge into abstract humanity. In Eliot's verse a comparison of one character with another is often, to a degree unusual even in poetry, an identification; because of the scanty individuation, the distinctions between persons and between levels of actuality are unstable. Agamemnon appears not merely as a figure comparable to Sweeney; he *is* Sweeney, or at least the two men are not altogether distinct. The Women in *The Waste Land* are all one woman, as Eliot tells us plainly, the men all one man, and "the two sexes meet in Tiresias," who is man in the archetypal role of quester.

Personality is shadowy and tentative; the human, not the individual, occupies almost all the poet's attention. The characters are like unconscious immortals who, in the fashion of Tiresias, change shape, setting, culture from age to age and repeatedly perform the same ritualistic functions in Egypt, in Greece, in England, from behind masks that betray nothing of the distinctive face.

Among all the possible roles, Eliot has chosen mainly to portray that of the quester, man in his role as seeker for meaning, truth, reality, virtue, the good life. All the events of Eliot's verse take their meaning from their relationship to this quest, and all the characters must be interpreted according to the ways in which they fulfill this role. Those who continue to pursue the goal either have or do not have the requisite qualifications; those who fail to pursue it at all, or who give up the pursuit, are damned. Virtually every character can be evaluated in terms of his reference to this central situation. Since the pursuit may be attempted through various human activities —mainly love, poetry, political and economic activity (history), and religion—some characters are treated only or mainly in terms of the search as it may be made through one of these areas. Most of the women of *The Waste Land,* for example, are reprehensible for their degrading attitudes toward human love, which in Eliot's verse never turns out to be a very profitable path for the quester. The quester in *Ash Wednesday* works through religion, in *Four Quartets* through several of the possible activities, but in *The Waste Land* the protagonist's search is more general: it is *the* quest, whatever its specific form.

Critiques

I. A. Richards

. . . The charge most usually brought against Mr. Eliot's poetry is that it is overintellectualized. One reason for this is his use of allusion. A reader who in one short poem picks up allusions to *The Aspern Papers, Othello,* "A Toccata of Galuppi's," Marston, *The Phoenix and the Turtle, Antony and Cleopatra* (twice), "The Extasie," *Macbeth, The Merchant of Venice,* and Ruskin, feels that his wits are being unusually well exercised. He may easily leap to the conclusion that the basis of the poem is in wit also. But this would be a mistake. These things come in, not that the reader may be ingenious or admire the writer's erudition (this last accusation has tempted several critics to disgrace themselves), but for the sake of the emotional aura which they bring and the attitudes they incite. Allusion in Mr. Eliot's hands is a technical device for compression. *The Waste Land* is the equivalent in content to an epic. Without this device twelve books would have been needed. But these allusions and the notes in which some of them are elucidated have made many a petulant reader turn down his thumb at once. Such a reader has not begun to understand what it is all about.

This objection is connected with another, that of obscurity. To quote a recent pronouncement upon *The Waste Land* from Mr. Middleton Murry: "The reader is compelled, in the mere effort to understand, to adopt an attitude of intellectual suspicion, which makes impossible the communication of feeling. The work offends against the most elementary canon of good writing: that the immediate effect should be unambiguous." Consider first this "canon." What would happen, if we pressed it, to Shakespeare's greatest sonnets or to *Hamlet?* The truth is that very much of the best poetry is necessarily ambiguous in its immediate effect. Even the most careful and responsive reader must reread and do hard work before the poem forms

From "The Poetry of T. S. Eliot," in Principles of Literary Criticism, *by I. A. Richards. (New York: Harcourt, Brace & World, Inc.; London: Routledge & Kegan Paul Ltd., 1934), pp. 290–92. Copyright © 1934 by Harcourt, Brace & World, Inc., and Routledge & Kegan Paul Ltd. Reprinted by permission of the publishers.*

itself clearly and unambiguously in his mind. An original poem, as much as a new branch of mathematics, compels the mind which receives it to grow, and this takes time. Anyone who upon reflection asserts the contrary for his own case must be either a demigod or dishonest; probably Mr. Murry was in haste. His remarks show that he has failed in his attempt to read the poem, and they reveal, in part, the reason for his failure—namely, his own overintellectual approach. To read it successfully he would have to discontinue his present self-mystifications.

The critical question in all cases is whether the poem is worth the trouble it entails. For *The Waste Land* this is considerable. There is Miss Weston's *From Ritual to Romance* to read, and its "astral" trimmings to be discarded—they have nothing to do with Mr. Eliot's poem. There is Canto XXVI of the *Purgatorio* to be studied—the relevance of the close of that canto to the whole of Mr. Eliot's work must be insisted upon. It illuminates his persistent concern with sex, the problem of our generation, as religion was the problem of the last. There is the central position of Tiresias in the poem to be puzzled out—the cryptic form of the note which Mr. Eliot writes on this point is just a little tiresome. It is a way of underlining the fact that the poem is concerned with many aspects of the one fact of sex, a hint that is perhaps neither indispensable nor entirely successful.

When all this has been done by the reader, when the materials with which the words are to clothe themselves have been collected, the poem still remains to be read. And it is easy to fail in this undertaking. An "attitude of intellectual suspicion" must certainly be abandoned. But this is not difficult to those who still know how to give their feelings precedence to their thoughts, who can accept and unify an experience without trying to catch it in an intellectual net or to squeeze out a doctrine. One form of this attempt must be mentioned. Some, misled no doubt by its origin in a Mystery, have endeavoured to give the poem a symbolical reading. But its symbols are not mystical, but emotional. They stand, that is, not for ineffable objects, but for normal human experience. The poem, in fact, is radically naturalistic; only its compression makes it appear otherwise. And in this it probably comes nearer to the original Mystery which it perpetuates than transcendentalism does.

Stephen Spender

I. A. Richards has said that in *The Waste Land* T. S. Eliot has effected a "severance between his poetry and *all* beliefs." . . . " 'In the destructive element immerse. That is the way.' "

I think that the last lines of "The Fire Sermon" section, "O Lord thou pluckest me out" are not "severed" from all belief. But what Eliot most certainly has done is to immerse himself in the destructive element. In *The Waste Land* he has made an artistic whole out of fragments. The poem is not built on the blank verse or free verse meters which are the basis of its separate parts. The meter, so far from being architectural, helps to convey the sense of fragmentariness in the poem. For example, a few lines of the last section of "What the Thunder Said":

> Here is no water but only rock
> Rock and no water and the sandy road
> The road winding above among the mountains
> Which are mountains of rock without water
> If there were water we should stop and drink,

are not sequentially related to the mood and rhythm of "A Game of Chess." The lines I have quoted read like some fragment of rhetorical poetic drama: "A Game of Chess" surprises us by its sensual, romantic mood, and "Death by Water" may take the reader to the Greek Anthology. These fragments are not related to each other, but to the whole poem; they only contribute to each other in falling apart, and always suggesting to us that they are parts of something larger than their surroundings. We are reminded of a ruined city in which the parts are all disintegrated, yet still together form a whole. What remains in our minds is the whole poem, which is related to a series of fragments, not a series of fragments which are collected together to construct a whole poem.

Instead of a basis of accepted belief, the whole structure of Eliot's poem is based on certain primitive rituals and myths, which, he seems to feel, must be psychological certainties, being a part of what psychologists call our "race memory." He is appealing to scientific legend, where Yeats appeals to poetic legend. The authority behind *The*

Stephen Spender, The Destructive Element (Boston: Houghton Mifflin Company, 1936), pp. 144–47. Copyright 1936 by Stephen Spender. Reprinted by permission of the Houghton Mifflin Company, Jonathan Cape, Ltd., A. D. Peters, Ltd., and Harold Matson Company, Inc.

Waste Land is not the Catholic Church, nor romantic lore, but anthropology from the volumes of Sir James Frazer's *The Golden Bough*. Eliot has tried to indicate, beneath the very ephemeral and violent movements of our own civilization, the gradual and magical contours of man's earliest religious beliefs. The effect he sets out to achieve is illustrated by Freud's remark in *Civilization and its Discontents* that the growth of the individual mind resembles the growth of Rome, supposing that modern Rome, as it is today, were coexistent with the buildings of Rome at every period in her history; and that beneath the modern architecture was found the architecture of every earlier period, in a perfect state of preservation.

The method of *The Waste Land* is justified insofar as it fulfils the psychological truth observed by Freud. But Eliot's way of doing this is perhaps a little too studied. The poem seems to lean rather too heavily on Sir James Frazer, and *The Golden Bough* tends to form a private poem concealed in the real poem, in the same way as Joyce's private poem about the Odyssey is enshrined in *Ulysses*. The work is very slightly tainted by the learning of the Cambridge don. Perhaps the main reason for this is that, although Eliot's attitude is much more objective and generalized in *The Waste Land* than in any earlier poem, the psychology of his people is just as crude. His ladies, his bank clerks, his Sweeneys, his Mrs. Porters, his pub conversationalists, are all part of the world of *things*. Psychologically they are far cruder than the Babbitts and other creations of Sinclair Lewis. One of the most astonishing things about Eliot is that a poet with such a strong dramatic style should seem so blinded to the existence of people outside himself. Yet the effect of his poetry depends very largely on this blindness.

Eliot seems to think, quite rightly, that what makes people living is their beliefs. But to him it seems impossible to accept any belief that is not a religious belief: one either rejects all belief, as I. A. Richards finds he has done in *The Waste Land,* or else one accepts a religious belief in salvation and damnation. Those who do not accept this belief are not even damned, but eternally dead. For that reason, the people about whom he writes in his poems are dead, because they are not allowed to hold with any conviction the small private beliefs which are as many as people's separate occupations. There is a whole list of such beliefs in St. J. Perse's *Anabase,* a poem which Eliot himself has translated: "He who sees his soul reflected in a blade; the man learned in sciences, in onomastic; the well thought of in councils, he who names fountains," etc. These are the living: yet they seem to be shut out of Eliot's poetry, because "to see his

soul reflected in a blade" puts a man outside the pale even of the
damned.

B. Rajan

When Pound dissuaded Eliot from making "Gerontion" a part of
The Waste Land, he could not have been aware of the evolving
logic of the *oeuvre.* Nevertheless, his action contributed to that logic.
"Gerontion" looks forward to *The Waste Land* if only because there
must be a world at the bottom of Dover cliff. Gerontion himself is
unable to enter that world. His monologue, made up of the thoughts
"of a dry brain in a dry season," is carefully distanced from experience, and even the encounter to which he reaches imaginatively
cannot be totally faced. To go forward from this point is to enter
the abyss and to be prepared to prove nothingness on one's pulses.
When one accepts the risk one also discovers that the risk is the only
possibility of survival.

Seen in the symbolic continuum, the waste land is Prufrock's world
more fully realized, a world where prophecy has fallen to fortune-
telling, where love has hardened into the expertise of lust, where
April is the cruellest month, and where the dead are no longer buried,
but planted in gardens. The fifth section is a break-out from this
world, the dimensions of which are carefully controlled to fall short
of a breakthrough. Because survival cannot be preached, but only
endured, the mythologizing structure is crucially important in en-
suring that whatever progress is achieved is not simply talked about,
but lived through imaginatively. What the thunder says is the result
of what the poem becomes, though, for reasons which will be apparent, the thunder speaks as a voice sought for by the poem but re-
maining outside it.

The Waste Land does not end where it begins. It may return to
where it started with deeper understanding, but the mytho-dramatic
progress is not depicted as circular. A journey to Chapel Perilous is
undertaken, delirium and near-death evoke an ancient experience, a
damp gust brings rain from which the leaves are limp, the thunder
speaks, proclaiming oracularly the conditions for deliverance, and
the protagonist ends, fishing on the shore with the arid plain behind

*From "The Overwhelming Question," by B. Rajan. Sewanee Review, LXXIV
(Winter 1966), 367–68. Copyright © 1966 by the University of the South. Reprinted
by permission of the* Sewanee Review.

him. These are small gains but their very narrowness suggests their authenticity. As for the thunder, its pronouncements are designed to leave one in what Eliot once called a state of enlightened mystification. Oracles achieve validity rather than clarity, and what they mean is decided by how experience reads them. One strong note in the voice of this oracle is a call to commitment—the awful daring of a moment's surrender, the recognition of the self as a prison, and the sea that would have been calm if one had chosen to venture on it, all seem to point straightforwardly in the same direction. When the protagonist decides to set his lands in order, as the bridges of the unreal city fall about him, we are witnessing the recovery of a traditional understanding. The collapse of civilization which a superficial reading (abetted by Eliot's notes) invites us to see here is also the death of an illusion, and reality can be born only from inward renewal.

The thunder speaks from the horizon of *The Waste Land* because what it has to say is discerned rather than experienced. The break-out from sterility is no more than that; it is not a movement into fruitfulness. The poem is an advance from "Gerontion," building on that poem's terrified recognitions and taking the vital step forward from a condition in which neither fear nor courage can save us. Its conclusion sets the arid plain behind and moves us to the fringe of a world which the poem can formulate but cannot enter. To make that entrance is the function of *Ash Wednesday*.

F. O. Matthiessen

. . . In case there should be some feeling that either Joyce or Eliot has revealed a kind of bookish weakness in turning for his structure to literature rather than to life, it should be recollected that Shakespeare himself created hardly any of his plots, and that by the very fact of taking ready-made the pattern of his characters' actions, he could devote his undivided attention to endowing them with life. It is only an uninformed prejudice which holds that literature must start from actual personal experience. It certainly must end with giving a sense of life; but it is not at all necessary that the poet should have undergone in his own person what he describes. Indeed, the more catholic the range of the artist, the more obviously impossible that would be. The poet's imagination can work as well on his reading as on the raw material of his senses. It is a mark of human maturity, as Eliot noted in his discussion of the metaphysical poets, that there should not be a separation in an individual's sensibility between reading and experience any more than between emotion and thought.

R. G. Collingwood

The decay of our civilization, as depicted in *The Waste Land*, is not an affair of violence and wrong-doing. It is not exhibited in the persecution of the virtuous and in the flourishing of the wicked like a green bay tree. It is not even a triumph of the meaner sins, avarice and lust. The drowned Phoenician sailor has forgotten the profit and loss; the rape of Philomel by the barbarous king is only a carved picture, a withered stump of time. These things are for remembrance, to contrast with a present where nothing is but stony rubbish, dead tree, dry rock, revealed in their nakedness by an April that breeds lilacs out of the dead land, but no new life in the dead heart of man. There is no question here of expressing private emotions; the picture to be painted is not the picture of any individual, or of any individual shadow, however lengthened into spurious history by morning or evening sun; it is the picture of a whole world of men, shadows themselves, flowing over London Bridge in the winter fog of that Limbo which involves those who, because they never lived, are equally hateful to God and to his enemies.

The picture unrolls. First the rich, the idle man and his idle mistress, surrounded by all the apparatus of luxury and learning; but in their hearts there is not even 'lust, nothing but fretted nerves and the exasperation of boredom. Then the public-house at night; the poor, no less empty-hearted: idle recrimination, futile longing for a good time, barren wombs and faded, fruitless youth, and an awful anonymous voice punctuating the chatter with a warning "Hurry up please it's time." Time for all these things to end; time's winged chariot, the grave a fine and private place, and mad Ophelia's goodnight, the river waiting for her. And then the river itself, with its memories of idle summer love-making, futile passionless seductions, the lover whose vanity makes a welcome of indifference, the mistress brought up to expect nothing; with contrasting memories of the splendors once created by Sir Christopher Wren, the pageantry of Elizabeth, and Saint Augustine for whom lust was real and a thing worth fighting.

Enough of detail. The poem depicts a world where the wholesome flowing water of emotion, which alone fertilizes all human activity, has dried up. Passions that once ran so strongly as to threaten the defeat of prudence, the destruction of human individuality, the wreck of men's little ships, are shrunk to nothing. No one gives; no one will risk himself by sympathizing; no one has anything to control. We are imprisoned in ourselves, becalmed in a windless selfishness. The only emotion left us is fear: fear of emotion itself, fear of death by drowning in it, fear in a handful of dust.

This poem is not in the least amusing. Nor is it in the least magical. The reader who expects it to be satire, or an entertaining description of vices, is as disappointed with it as the reader who expects it to be propaganda, or an exhortation to get up and do something. To the annoyance of both parties, it contains no indictments and no proposals. To the amateurs of literature, brought up on the idea of poetry as a genteel amusement, the thing is an affront. To the little neo-Kiplings who think of poetry as an incitement to political virtue, it is even worse; for it describes an evil where no one and nothing is to blame, an evil not curable by shooting capitalists or destroying a social system, a disease which has so eaten into civilization that political remedies are about as useful as poulticing a cancer.

To readers who want not amusement or magic, but poetry, and who want to know what poetry can be, if it is to be neither of these things, *The Waste Land* supplies an answer. And by reflecting on it we can perhaps detect one more characteristic which art must have, if it is to forgo both entertainment value and magical value, and draw a subject matter from its audience themselves. It must be prophetic. The artist must prophesy not in the sense that he foretells things to come, but in the sense that he tells his audience, at risk of their displeasure, the secrets of their own hearts. His business as an artist is to speak out, to make a clean breast. But what he has to utter is not, as the individualistic theory of art would have us think, his own secrets. As spokesman of his community, the secrets he must utter are theirs. The reason why they need him is that no community altogether knows its own heart; and by failing in this knowledge a community deceives itself on the one subject concerning which ignorance means death. For the evils which come from that ignorance the poet as prophet suggests no remedy, because he has already given one. The remedy is the poem itself. Art is the community's medicine for the worst disease of mind, the corruption of consciousness.

PART TWO

Essays

An Anatomy of Melancholy

by Conrad Aiken

Prefatory Note

The review of *The Waste Land,* with the above title, came out in *The New Republic* on February 7, 1923, in other words, four months after the poem's appearance in *The Criterion* of October 1922; and I suspect it was the first full-length favorable review the poem had then received—at any rate, I do not remember any predecessors. To be sure, I had the advantage of having known Eliot intimately for fifteen years—since my freshman year at Harvard—and had already, in 1917 and 1921, apropos of *Prufrock* and *The Sacred Wood,* heralded him as the fugleman of many things to come. Of *Prufrock* I said that in its wonderfully varied use of rhymed free verse there was a probable solution of the quarrel, at that time as violent as it is now, about the usefulness of rhyme or verse at all: the Imagists, and Others, including of course Williams and his eternal Object, were already hard at it. I think *Prufrock* still has its way.

As to *The Waste Land* and my review, it might be helpful for the general picture if I record here two episodes with Eliot, one before he had written the poem, and one after.

In the winter of 1921–22 I was in London, living in Bayswater, and Eliot and myself lunched together two or three times a week in the City, near his bank: thus resuming a habit we had formed many years before, in Cambridge. He always had with him his pocket edition of Dante. And of course we discussed the literary scene, with some acerbity and hilarity, and with the immense advantage of being outsiders (though both of us were already contributing to the English reviews); discussing also the then-just-beginning possibility of *The*

Conrad Aiken, A Reviewer's ABC *(New York: Meridian Books, Inc., 1958), pp. 176-81.* Copyright © *1958 by Conrad Aiken. Reprinted by permission of Brandt & Brandt.*

Criterion, through the generosity of Lady Rothermere. And it was at one of these meetings, in midwinter, that he told me one day, and with visible concern, that although every evening he went home to his flat hoping that he could start writing again, and with every confidence that the material was *there* and waiting, night after night the hope proved illusory: the sharpened pencil lay unused by the untouched sheet of paper. What could be the matter? He didn't know. He asked me if *I* had ever experienced any such thing. And of course my reply that I hadn't wasn't calculated to make him feel any happier.

But it worried me, as it worried him. And so, not unnaturally, I mentioned it to a very good friend of mine, Dilston Radcliffe, who was at that time being analyzed by the remarkable American lay analyst, Homer Lane. Radcliffe, himself something of a poet, was at once very much interested, and volunteered, at his next meeting with Lane, to ask him what he thought of it. And a few days later came the somewhat startling answer from Lane: "Tell your friend Aiken to tell *his* friend Eliot that all that's stopping him is his fear of putting anything down that is short of perfection. He thinks he's God."

The result was, I suppose, foreseeable, though I didn't foresee it. For when I told Eliot of Lane's opinion, he was literally speechless with rage, both at Lane and myself. The *intrusion,* quite simply, was one that was intolerable. But ever since I have been entirely convinced that it did the trick, it broke the log-jam. A month or two later he went to Switzerland, and there wrote *The Waste Land.*

Which in due course appeared in the first issue of *The Criterion,* by that time endowed by Lady Rothermere, and again in due course came to me from *The New Republic,* for review. And once more, it was as we proceeded from Lloyd's bank to our favorite pub, by the Cannon Street Station, for grilled rump steak and a pint of Bass, that another explosion occurred.

For I said, "You know, I've called my long review of your poem 'An Anatomy of Melancholy.' "

He turned on me with that icy fury of which he alone was capable, and said fiercely: "There is nothing melancholy about it!"

To which I in turn replied: "The reference, Tom, was to BURTON's *Anatomy of Melancholy,* and the quite extraordinary amount of *quotation* it contains!"

The joke was acceptable, and we both roared with laughter.

To all of which I think I need add one small regret about that review. How could I mention that I had long been familiar with such passages as "A woman drew her long black hair out tight," which I had seen as poems, or part-poems, in themselves? And now saw inserted into *The Waste Land* as into a mosaic. This would be to make use of private knowledge, a betrayal. Just the same, it should perhaps have been done, and the conclusion drawn: that they were not *organically* a part of the total meaning.

*   *   *

Mr. T. S. Eliot is one of the most individual of contemporary poets, and at the same time, anomalously, one of the most "traditional." By individual I mean that he can be, and often is (distressingly, to some), aware in his own way; as when he observes of a woman (in "Rhapsody on a Windy Night") that the door "opens on her like a grin" and that the corner of her eye "Twists like a crooked pin." Everywhere, in the very small body of his work, is similar evidence of a delicate sensibility, somewhat shrinking, somewhat injured, and always sharply itself. But also, with this capacity or necessity for being aware in his own way, Mr. Eliot has a haunting, a tyrannous awareness that there have been many other awarenesses before; and that the extent of his own awareness, and perhaps even the nature of it, is a consequence of these. He is, more than most poets, conscious of his roots. If this consciousness had not become acute in "Prufrock" or the "Portrait of a Lady," it was nevertheless probably there: and the roots were quite conspicuously French, and dated, say, 1870–1900. A little later, as his sense of the past had become more pressing, it seemed that he was positively redirecting his roots—urging them to draw a morbid dramatic sharpness from Webster and Donne, a faded dry gilt of cynicism and formality from the Restoration. This search of the tomb produced "Sweeney" and "Whispers of Immortality." And finally, in *The Waste Land,* Mr. Eliot's sense of the literary past has become so overmastering as almost to constitute the motive of the work. It is as if, in conjunction with the Mr. Pound of the *Cantos,* he wanted to make a "literature of literature"—a poetry actuated not more by life itself than by poetry; as if he had concluded that the characteristic awareness of a poet of the twentieth century must inevitably, or ideally, be a very complex and very literary awareness, able to speak only, or best, in terms of the literary past, the terms which had molded its tongue. This involves a kind of idolatry of literature with which it is a little difficult to sympathize. In positing, as it seems to, that there is nothing left for literature to do but become a kind of parasitic growth on literature, a sort of mistletoe, it involves, I think, a definite astigmatism—a distortion. But the theory is interesting if only because it has colored an important and brilliant piece of work.

The Waste Land is unquestionably important, unquestionably brilliant. It is important partly because its 433 lines summarize Mr. Eliot, for the moment, and demonstrate that he is an even better poet than most had thought; and partly because it embodies the theory just touched upon, the theory of the "allusive" method in poetry. *The Waste Land* is, indeed, a poem of allusion all compact. It purports to be symbolical; most of its symbols are drawn from literature or legend; and Mr. Eliot has thought it necessary to supply, in notes, a list of the many quotations, references, and translations with which it bristles. He observes candidly that the poem presents "difficulties," and requires "elucidation." This serves to raise, at once, the question whether these difficulties, in which perhaps Mr. Eliot takes a little pride, are so much the result of complexity, a fine elaborateness, as of confusion. The poem has been compared, by one reviewer, to a "full-rigged ship built in a bottle," the suggestion being that it is a perfect piece of construction. But is it a perfect piece of construction? Is the complex material mastered, and made coherent? Or, if the poem is not successful in that way, in what way *is* it successful? Has it the formal and intellectual complex unity of a microscopic *Divine Comedy;* or is its unity—supposing it to have one—of another sort?

If we leave aside for the moment all other consideration, and read the poem solely with the intention of understanding, with the aid of notes, the symbolism; of making out what it is that is symbolized, and how these symbolized feelings are brought into relation with each other and with other matters in the poem; I think we must, with reservations, and with no invidiousness, conclude that the poem is not, in any formal sense, coherent. We cannot feel that all the symbolisms belong quite inevitably where they have been put; that the order of the parts is an inevitable order; that there is anything more than a rudimentary progress from one theme to another; nor that the relation between the more symbolic parts and the less is always as definite as it should be. What we feel is that Mr. Eliot has not wholly annealed the allusive matter, has left it unabsorbed, lodged in gleaming fragments amid material alien to it. Again, there is a distinct weakness consequent on the use of allusions which may have both intellectual and emotional value for Mr. Eliot, but (even with the notes) none for us. The "Waste Land" of the Grail Legend might be a good symbol, if it were something with which we were sufficiently familiar. But it can never, even when explained, be a good symbol, simply because it has no immediate associations for us. It might, of course, be a good *theme*. In that case it would be given us. But Mr. Eliot uses it for purposes of overtone; he refers to it; and as overtone it quite clearly fails. He gives us, superbly, *a* waste land—

not *the* waste land. Why, then, refer to the latter at all—if he is not, in the poem, really going to use it? Hyacinth fails in the same way. So does the Fisher King. So does the Hanged Man, which Mr. Eliot tells us he associates with Frazer's Hanged God—we take his word for it. But if the precise association is worth anything, it is worth putting into the poem; otherwise there can be no purpose in mentioning it. Why, again, Datta, Dayadhvam, Damyata? Or Shantih? Do they not say a good deal less for us than "Give: sympathize: control" or "Peace"? Of course; but Mr. Eliot replies that he wants them not merely to mean those particular things, but also to mean them in a particular way—that is, to be remembered in connection with a Upanishad. Unfortunately, we have none of us this memory, nor can he give it to us; and in the upshot he gives us only a series of agreeable sounds which might as well have been nonsense. What we get at, and I think it is important, is that in none of these particular cases does the reference, the allusion, justify itself intrinsically, make itself felt. When we are aware of these references at all (sometimes they are unidentifiable) we are aware of them simply as something unintelligible but suggestive. When they have been explained, we are aware of the material referred to, the fact (for instance, a vegetation ceremony), as something useless for our enjoyment or understanding of the poem, something distinctly "dragged in," and only, perhaps, of interest as having suggested a pleasantly ambiguous line. For unless an allusion is made to live identifiably, to flower where transplanted, it is otiose. We admit the beauty of the implicational or allusive method; but the key to an implication should be in the implication itself, not outside of it. We admit the value of the esoteric pattern; but the pattern should disclose its secret, should not be dependent on a cypher. Mr. Eliot assumes for his allusions, and for the fact that they actually allude to something, an importance which the allusions themselves do not, as expressed, aesthetically command, nor, as explained, logically command; which is pretentious. He is a little pretentious, too, in his "plan"—*qui pourtant n'existe pas.* If it is a plan, then its principle is oddly akin to planlessness. Here and there, in the wilderness, a broken finger-post.

I enumerate these objections not, I must emphasize, in derogation of the poem, but to dispel, if possible, an illusion as to its nature. It is perhaps important to note that Mr. Eliot, with his comment on the "plan," and several critics, with their admiration of the poem's woven complexity, minister to the idea that *The Waste Land* is, precisely, a kind of epic in a walnut shell: elaborate, ordered, unfolded with a logic at every joint discernible; but it is also important to note that this idea is false. With or without the notes the poem belongs rather to that symbolical order in which one may justly say that the "meaning" is not explicitly, or exactly, worked out. Mr. Eliot's net is wide, its meshes are small; and he catches a good deal more—thank heaven—than he pretends to. If space permitted one could pick out many lines and passages and parodies and quotations which do not demonstrably, in any "logical" sense, carry forward the theme, passages which unjustifiably, but happily, "expand" beyond its purpose. Thus the poem has an emotional value far clearer and richer than its arbitrary and rather unworkable logical value. One might assume that it originally consisted of a number of separate poems which have been telescoped—given a kind of forced unity. The Waste Land conception offered itself as a generous net which would, if not unify, at any rate contain these varied elements. We are aware of this superficial "binding"—we observe the anticipation and repetition of themes, motifs; "Fear death by water" anticipates the episode of Phlebas, the cry of the nightingale is repeated; but these are pretty flimsy links, and do not genuinely bind because they do not reappear naturally, but arbitrarily. This suggests, indeed, that Mr. Eliot is perhaps attempting a kind of program music in words, endeavoring to rule out "emotional accidents" by supplying his readers, in notes, with only those associations which are correct. He himself hints at the musical analogy when he observes that "In the first part of Part V three themes are employed."

I think, therefore, that the poem must be taken—most invitingly offers itself—as a brilliant and kaleidoscopic confusion; as a series of sharp, discrete, slightly related perceptions and feelings, dramatically and lyrically presented, and violently juxtaposed (for effect of dissonance), so as to give us an impression of an intensely modern, intensely literary consciousness which perceives itself to be not a unit but a chance correlation or conglomerate of mutually discolorative fragments. We are invited into a mind, a world, which is a "broken bundle of mirrors," a "heap of broken images." Isn't it that Mr. Eliot, finding it "impossible to say just what he means"—to recapitulate, to enumerate all the events and discoveries and memories that make a consciousness—has emulated the "magic lantern" that throws "the nerves in pattern on a screen"? If we perceive the poem in this light, as a series of brilliant, brief, unrelated or dimly related pictures by which a consciousness empties itself of its characteristic contents, then we also perceive that, anomalously, though the dropping out of any one picture would not in the least affect the logic or "meaning" of the whole, it would seriously detract from the value of the portrait. The "plan" of the poem would not greatly suffer, one makes bold to assert, by the elimination of "April is the cruellest month" or Phlebas,

or the Thames daughters, or Sosostris or "You gave me hyacinths" or
"A woman drew her long black hair out tight"; nor would it matter
if it did. These things are not important parts of an important or
careful intellectual pattern; but they are important parts of an important emotional ensemble. The relations between Tiresias (who is
said to unify the poem, in a sense, as spectator) and the Waste Land,
or Mr. Eugenides, or Hyacinth, or any other fragment, is a dim and
tonal one, not exact. It will not bear analysis, it is not always operating, nor can one say with assurance, at any given point, how much
it is operating. In this sense *The Waste Land* is a series of separate
poems or passages, not perhaps all written at one time or with one
aim, to which a spurious but happy sequence has been given. This
spurious sequence has a value—it creates the necessary superficial
formal unity; but it need not be stressed, as the Notes stress it. Could
one not wholly rely for one's unity—as Mr. Eliot *has* largely relied—
simply on the dim unity of "personality" which would underlie the
retailed contents of a single consciousness? Unless one is going to
carry unification very far, weave and interweave very closely, it would
perhaps be as well not to unify it at all; to dispense, for example,
with arbitrary repetitions.

We reach thus the conclusion that the poem succeeds—as it bril-
liantly does—by virtue of its incoherence, not of its plan; by virtue
of its ambiguities, not of its explanations. Its incoherence is a virtue
because its *donnée* is incoherence. Its rich, vivid, crowded use of
implication is a virtue, as implication is always a virtue—it shimmers,
it suggests, it gives the desired strangeness. But when, as often, Mr.
Eliot uses an implication beautifully—conveys by means of a picture-
symbol or action-symbol a feeling—we do not require to be told that
he had in mind a passage in the *Encyclopedia,* or the color of his
nursery wall; the information is disquieting, has a sour air of ped-
antry. We "accept" the poem as we would accept a powerful, melancholy tone-poem. We do not want to be told what occurs; nor is it
more than mildly amusing to know what passages are, in the Straussian
manner, echoes or parodies. We cannot believe that every syllable
has an algebraic inevitability, nor would we wish it so. We could
dispense with the French, Italian, Latin, and Hindu phrases—they
are irritating. But when our reservations have all been made, we
accept *The Waste Land* as one of the most moving and original
poems of our time. It captures us. And we sigh, with a dubious eye
on the "notes" and "plan," our bewilderment that after so fine a
performance Mr. Eliot should have thought it an occasion for calling
"Tullia's ape a marmosyte." Tullia's ape is good enough.

The Waste Land: Critique of the Myth

by Cleanth Brooks

Though much has been written on *The Waste Land,* it will not be difficult to show that most of its critics misconceive entirely the theme and the structure of the poem. There has been little or no attempt to deal with it as a unified whole. F. R. Leavis and F. O. Matthiessen have treated large sections of the poem in detail, and I am obviously indebted to both of them. I believe, however, that Leavis makes some positive errors of interpretation. I find myself in almost complete agreement with Matthiessen in his commentary on the sections which he deals with in his *Achievement of T. S. Eliot,* but the plan of his book does not allow for a complete consecutive examination of the poem.

In view of the state of criticism with regard to the poem, it is best for us to approach it frankly on the basis of its theme. I prefer, however, not to raise just here the question of how important it is for the reader to have an explicit intellectual account of the various symbols and a logical account of their relationships. It may well be that such rationalization is no more than a scaffolding to be got out of the way before we contemplate the poem itself as poem. But many readers (including myself) find the erection of such a scaffolding valuable— if not absolutely necessary—and if some readers will be tempted to lay more stress upon the scaffolding than they should, there are perhaps still more readers who, without the help of such a scaffolding, will be prevented from getting at the poem at all.

The basic symbol used, that of the waste land, is taken of course, from Miss Jessie Weston's *From Ritual to Romance.* In the legends which she treats there, the land has been blighted by a curse. The crops do not grow and the animals cannot reproduce. The plight of the land is summed up by, and connected with, the plight of the lord of the land, the Fisher King, who has been rendered impotent by

Cleanth Brooks, "The Waste Land: Critique of the Myth," *from* Modern Poetry and the Tradition, *pp. 136–72. Copyright, 1939, by the University of North Carolina Press, Chapel Hill, North Carolina. Reprinted by permission of the publisher.*

maiming or sickness. The curse can be removed only by the appearance of a knight who will ask the meanings of the various symbols which are displayed to him in the castle. The shift in meaning from physical to spiritual sterility is easily made, and was, as a matter of fact, made in certain of the legends. As Eliot has pointed out, a knowledge of this symbolism is essential for an understanding of the poem.

Of hardly less importance to the reader, however, is a knowledge of Eliot's basic method. *The Waste Land* is built on a major contrast —a device which is a favorite of Eliot's and is to be found in many of his poems, particularly his later poems. The contrast is between two kinds of life and two kinds of death. Life devoid of meaning is death; sacrifice, even the sacrificial death, may be life-giving, an awakening to life. The poem occupies itself to a great extent with this paradox, and with a number of variations upon it.

Eliot has stated the matter quite explicitly himself in one of his essays. In his "Baudelaire" he says: "One aphorism which has been especially noticed is the following: *la volupté unique et suprême de l'amour gît dans la certitude de faire le mal.* This means, I think, that Baudelaire has perceived that what distinguishes the relations of man and woman from the copulation of beasts is the knowledge of Good and Evil (of *moral* Good and Evil which are not natural Good and Bad or puritan Right and Wrong). Having an imperfect, vague romantic conception of Good, he was at least able to understand that the sexual act as evil is more dignified, less boring, than as the natural, 'life-giving,' cheery automatism of the modern world. . . . So far as we are human, what we do must be either evil or good; so far as we do evil or good, we are human; and it is better, in a paradoxical way, to do evil than to do nothing: at least, *we exist* [italics mine— C.B.]." The last statement is highly important for an understanding of *The Waste Land.* The fact that men have lost the knowledge of good and evil, keeps them from being alive, and is the justification for viewing the modern waste land as a realm in which the inhabitants do not even exist.

This theme is stated in the quotation which prefaces the poem. The Sybil says: "I wish to die." Her statement has several possible interpretations. For one thing, she is saying what the pople who inhabit the waste land are saying. But she may also be saying what the speaker of "The Journey of the Magi" says: ". . . this Birth was/ Hard and bitter agony for us, like Death, our death./ . . . I should be glad of another death."

I

The first section of "The Burial of the Dead" develops the theme of the attractiveness of death, or of the difficulty in rousing oneself from the death in life in which the people of the waste land live. Men are afraid to live in reality. April, the month of rebirth, is not the most joyful season but the cruelest. Winter at least kept us warm in forgetful snow. The idea is one which Eliot has stressed elsewhere. Earlier in "Gerontion" he had written

> In the juvescence of the year
> Came Christ the tiger
> . . . .
> The tiger springs in the new year. Us he devours. . . .

More lately, in *Murder in the Cathedral,* he has the chorus say

> We do not wish anything to happen.
> Seven years we have lived quietly,
> Succeeded in avoiding notice,
> Living and partly living.

And in another passage: "Now I fear disturbance of the quiet seasons." Men dislike to be roused from their death-in-life.

The first part of "The Burial of the Dead" introduces this theme through a sort of reverie on the part of the protagonist—a reverie in which speculation on life glides off into memory of an actual conversation in the Hofgarten and back into speculation again. The function of the conversation is to establish the class and character of the protagonist. The reverie is resumed with line 19.

> What are the roots that clutch, what branches grow
> Out of this stony rubbish?

The protagonist answers for himself:

> Son of man,
> You cannot say, or guess, for you know only
> A heap of broken images, where the sun beats,
> And the dead tree gives no shelter, the cricket no relief,
> And the dry stone no sound of water.

In this passage there are references to Ezekiel and to Ecclesiastes, and these references indicate what it is that men no longer know: The passage referred to in Ezekiel 2, pictures a world thoroughly secularized:

1. And he said unto me, Son of man, stand upon thy feet, and I will speak unto thee.

2. And the spirit entered into me when he spake unto me, and set me upon my feet, that I heard him that spake unto me.

3. And he said unto me, Son of man, I send thee to the children of Israel, to a rebellious nation that hath rebelled against me: they and their fathers have transgressed against me, even unto this very day.

Other passages from Ezekiel are relevant to the poem, Chapter 37 in particular, which describes Ezekiel's waste land, where the prophet, in his vision of the valley of dry bones, contemplates the "burial of the dead" and is asked: "Son of man, can these bones live? And I answered, O Lord God, thou knowest. 4. Again he said unto me, Prophesy over these bones, and say unto them, O ye dry bones, hear the word of the Lord."

One of Ezekiel's prophecies was that Jerusalem would be conquered and the people led away into the Babylonian captivity. That captivity is alluded to in Section III of *The Waste Land,* line 182, where the Thames becomes the "waters of Leman."

The passage from Ecclesiastes 12, alluded to in Eliot's notes, describes the same sort of waste land:

1. Remember now thy Creator in the days of thy youth, while the evil days come not, nor the years draw nigh, when thou shalt say, I have no pleasure in them;

2. While the sun, or the light, or the moon, or the stars, be not darkened, nor the clouds return after the rain;

3. In the day when the keepers of the house shall tremble, and the strong men shall bow themselves, and the grinders cease because they are few, and those that look out of the windows be darkened,

4. And the doors shall be shut in the streets, when the sound of the grinding is low, and he shall rise up at the voice of the bird, and all the daughters of music shall be brought low;

5. Also when they shall be afraid of that which is high, and fears shall be in the way, and the almond tree shall flourish, and the grasshopper shall be a burden, *and desire shall fail* [italics mine]: because man goeth to his long home, and the mourners go about the streets;

6. Or ever the silver cord be loosed, or the golden bowl be broken, or

the pitcher be broken at the fountain, or the wheel broken at the cistern.

7. Then shall the dust return to the earth as it was: and the spirit shall return unto God who gave it.

8. Vanity of vanities, saith the preacher; all is vanity.

A reference to this passage is also evidently made in the nightmare vision of Section V of the poem.

The next section of "The Burial of the Dead" which begins with the scrap of song quoted from Wagner (perhaps another item in the reverie of the protagonist), states the opposite half of the paradox which underlies the poem: namely, that life at its highest moments of meaning and intensity resembles death. The song from Act I of Wagner's *Tristan und Isolde, "Frisch weht der Wind,"* is sung in the opera by a young sailor aboard the ship which is bringing Isolde to Cornwall. The *"Irisch kind"* of the song does not properly apply to Isolde at all. The song is merely one of happy and naïve love. It brings to the mind of the protagonist an experience of love—the vision of the hyacinth girl as she came back from the hyacinth garden. The poet says

> . . . my eyes failed, I was neither
> Living nor dead, and I knew nothing,
> Looking into the heart of light, the silence.

The line which immediately follows this passage, *"Oed' und leer das Meer,"* seems at first to be simply an extension of the last figure: that is, "Empty and wide the sea [of silence]." But the line, as a matter of fact, makes an ironic contrast; for the line, as it occurs in Act III of the opera, is the reply of the watcher who reports to the wounded Tristan that Isolde's ship is nowhere in sight; the sea is empty. And, though the *"Irisch kind"* of the first quotation is not Isolde, the reader familiar with the opera will apply it to Isolde when he comes to the line *"Oed' und leer das Meer."* For the question in the song is in essence Tristan's question in Act III: "My Irish child, where dwellest thou?" The two quotations from the opera which frame the ecstasy-of-love passage thus take on a new meaning in the altered context. In the first, love is happy; the boat rushes on with a fair wind behind it. In the second, love is absent; the sea is wide and empty. And the last quotation reminds us that even love cannot exist in the waste land.

The next passage, that in which Madame Sosostris figures, calls for further reference to Miss Weston's book. As Miss Weston has shown, the Tarot cards were originally used to determine the event of

highest importance to the people, the rising of the waters. Madame
Sosostris has fallen a long way from the high function of her predecessors. She is engaged merely in vulgar fortune-telling—is merely one
item in a generally vulgar civilization. But the symbols of the Tarot
pack are still unchanged. The various characters are still inscribed on
the cards, and she is reading in reality (though she does not know it)
the fortune of the protagonist. She finds that his card is that of the
drowned Phoenician Sailor, and so she warns him against death by
water, not realizing any more than do the other inhabitants of the
modern waste land that the way into life may be by death itself. The
drowned Phoenician Sailor is a type of the fertility god whose image
was thrown into the sea annually as a symbol of the death of summer.
As for the other figures in the pack: Belladonna, the Lady of the
Rocks, is woman in the waste land. The man with three staves, Eliot
says he associates rather arbitrarily with the Fisher King. The term
"arbitrarily" indicates that we are not to attempt to find a logical
connection here. (It may be interesting to point out, however, that
Eliot seems to have given, in a later poem, his reason for making the
association. In "The Hollow Men" he writes, speaking as one of the
Hollow Men:

> Let me also wear
> Such deliberate disguises
> Rat's coat, crowskin, crossed staves
> In a field
> Behaving as the wind behaves . . .

The figure is that of a scarecrow, fit symbol of the man who possesses
no reality, and fit type of the Fisher King, the maimed, impotent
king who ruled over the waste land of the legend. The man with
three staves in the deck of cards may thus have appealed to the poet
as an appropriate figure to which to assign the function of the Fisher
King, although the process of identification was too difficult to expect
the reader to follow and although knowledge of the process was not
necessary to an understanding of the poem.)

The Hanged Man, who represents the hanged god of Frazer (including the Christ), Eliot states in a note, is associated with the
hooded figure who appears in "What the Thunder Said." That he is
hooded accounts for Madame Sosostris' inability to see him; or rather,
here again the palaver of the modern fortune-teller is turned to new
and important account by the poet's shifting the reference into a new
and serious context. The Wheel and the one-eyed merchant will be
discussed later.

After the Madame Sosostris passage, Eliot proceeds to complicate his symbols for the sterility and unreality of the modern waste land by associating it with Baudelaire's *"fourmillante cité"* and with Dante's Limbo. The passages already quoted from Eliot's essay on Baudelaire will indicate one of the reasons why Baudelaire's lines are evoked here. In Baudelaire's city, dream and reality seem to mix, and it is interesting that Eliot in "The Hollow Men" refers to this same realm of death-in-life as "death's dream kingdom" in contradistinction to "death's other Kingdom."

The references to Dante are most important. The line, "I had not thought death had undone so many," is taken from the Third Canto of the *Inferno;* the line, "Sighs, short and infrequent, were exhaled," from the Fourth Canto. Mr. Matthiessen has already pointed out that the Third Canto deals with Dante's Limbo which is occupied by those who on earth had "lived without praise or blame." They share this abode with the angels "who were not rebels, nor were faithful to God, but were for themselves." They exemplify almost perfectly the secular attitude which dominates the modern world. Their grief, according to Dante, arises from the fact that they "have no hope of death; and their blind life is so debased, that they are envious of every other lot." But though they may not hope for death, Dante calls them "these wretches who never were alive." The people described in the Fourth Canto are those who lived virtuously but who died before the proclamation of the Gospel—they are the unbaptized. They form the second of the two classes of people who inhabit the modern waste land: those who are secularized and those who have no knowledge of the faith. Without a faith their life is in reality a death. To repeat the sentence from Eliot previously quoted: "So far as we do evil or good, we are human; and it is better, in a paradoxical way, to do evil than to do nothing: at least, we exist."

The Dante and Baudelaire references, then, come to the same thing as the allusion to the waste land of the medieval legends; and these various allusions, drawn from widely differing sources, enrich the comment on the modern city so that it becomes "unreal" on a number of levels: as seen through "the brown fog of a winter dawn"; as the medieval waste land and Dante's Limbo and Baudelaire's Paris are unreal.

The reference to Stetson stresses again the connection between the modern London of the poem and Dante's hell. After the statement, "I could never have believed death had undone so many," follow the words, "After I had distinguished some among them, I saw and knew the shade of him who made, through cowardice, the great refusal." The protagonist, like Dante, sees among the inhabitants of the contemporary waste land one whom he recognizes. (The name "Stetson" I take to have no ulterior significance. It is merely an ordinary name such as might be borne by the friend one might see in a crowd in a great city.) Mylae, as Mr. Matthiessen has pointed out, is the name of a battle between the Romans and the Carthaginians in the Punic War. The Punic War was a trade war—might be considered a rather close parallel to our late war. At any rate, it is plain that Eliot in having the protagonist address the friend in a London street as one who was with him in the Punic War rather than as one who was with him in the World War is making the point that all the wars are one war; all experience, one experience. As Eliot put the idea in *Murder in the Cathedral:*

> We do not know very much of the future
> Except that from generation to generation
> The same things happen again and again

I am not sure that Leavis and Matthiessen are correct in inferring that the line, "That corpse you planted last year in your garden," refers to the attempt to bury a memory. But whether or not this is true, the line certainly refers also to the buried god of the old fertility rites. It also is to be linked with the earlier passage—"What are the roots that clutch, what branches grow," etc. This allusion to the buried god will account for the ironical, almost taunting tone of the passage. The burial of the dead is now a sterile planting—without hope. But the advice to "keep the Dog far hence," in spite of the tone, is, I believe, well taken and serious. The passage in Webster goes as follows

> But keep the wolf far thence, that's foe to men,
> For with his nails he'll dig them up again.

Why does Eliot turn the wolf into a dog? And why does he reverse the point of importance from the animal's normal hostility to men to its friendliness? If, as some critics have suggested, he is merely interested in making a reference to Webster's darkest play, why alter the line? I am inclined to take the Dog (the capital letter is Eliot's) as Humanitarianism [1] and the related philosophies which, in their concern for man, extirpate the supernatural—dig up the corpse of the

---

[1] The reference is perhaps more general still: it may include Naturalism, and Science in the popular conception as the new magic which will enable man to conquer his environment completely.

buried god and thus prevent the rebirth of life. For the general idea, see Eliot's essay, "The Humanism of Irving Babbitt."

The last line of "The Burial of the Dead"—"You! hypocrite lecteur! mon semblable,—mon frère!" the quotation from Baudelaire, completes the universalization of Stetson begun by the reference to Mylae. Stetson is every man including the reader and Mr. Eliot himself.

II

If "The Burial of the Dead" gives the general abstract statement of the situation, the second part of *The Waste Land,* "A Game of Chess," gives a more concrete illustration. The easiest contrast in this section—and one which may easily blind the casual reader to a continued emphasis on the contrast between the two kinds of life, or the two kinds of death, already commented on—is the contrast between life in a rich and magnificent setting, and life in the low and vulgar setting of a London pub. But both scenes, however antithetical they may appear superficially, are scenes taken from the contemporary waste land. In both of them life has lost its meaning.

I am particularly indebted to Mr. Allen Tate's comment on the first part of this section. To quote from him, "The woman . . . is, I believe, the symbol of man at the present time. He is surrounded by the grandeurs of the past, but he does not participate in them; they don't sustain him." And to quote from another section of his commentary: "The rich experience of the great tradition depicted in the room receives a violent shock in contrast with a game that symbolizes the inhuman abstraction of the modern mind." Life has no meaning; history has no meaning; there is no answer to the question: "What shall we ever do?" The only thing that has meaning is the abstract game which they are to play, a game in which the meaning is assigned and arbitrary, meaning by convention only—in short, a game of chess.

This interpretation will account in part for the pointed reference to Cleopatra in the first lines of the section. But there is, I believe, a further reason for the poet's having compared the lady to Cleopatra. The queen in Shakespeare's drama—"Age cannot wither her, nor custom stale/Her infinite variety"—is perhaps the extreme exponent of love for love's sake, the feminine member of the pair of lovers who threw away an empire for love. But the infinite variety of the life of the woman in "A Game of Chess" *has* been staled. There is indeed no variety at all, and love simply does not exist. The function of the

sudden change in the description of the carvings and paintings in
the room from the heroic and magnificent to "and other withered
stumps of time" is obvious. But the reference to Philomela is particularly important, for Philomela, it seems to me, is one of the major
symbols of the poem.

Miss Weston points out (in *The Quest of the Holy Grail*) that a
section of one of the Grail manuscripts, which is apparently intended
to be a gloss on the Grail story, tells how the court of the rich Fisher
King was withdrawn from the knowledge of men when certain of
the maidens who frequented the shrine were raped and had their
golden cups taken from them. The curse on the land follows from
this act. Miss Weston conjectures that this may be a statement, in the
form of a parable, of the violation of the older mysteries which were
probably once celebrated openly, but were later forced underground.
Whether or not Mr. Eliot noticed this passage or intends a reference,
the violation of a woman makes a very good symbol of the process of
secularization. John Crowe Ransom makes the point very neatly for
us in *God Without Thunder*. Love is the aesthetic of sex; lust is the
science. Love implies a deferring of the satisfaction of the desire; it
implies a certain asceticism and a ritual. Lust drives forward urgently
and scientifically to the immediate extirpation of the desire. Our contemporary waste land is in large part the result of our scientific attitude—of our complete secularization. Needless to say, lust defeats its
own ends. The portrayal of "the change of Philomel, by the barbarous king" is a fitting commentary on the scene which it ornaments.
The waste land of the legend came in this way; the modern waste
land has come in this way.

This view is corroborated by the change of tense to which Edmund
Wilson has called attention: "And still she *cried,* and still the world
pursues [italics mine]." Apparently the "world" partakes in the barbarous king's action, and still partakes in that action.

To "dirty ears" the nightingale's song is not that which filled all
the desert with inviolable voice—it is "Jug Jug." Edmund Wilson has
pointed out that the rendition of the bird's song here represents not
merely the Elizabethans' neutral notation of the bird's song, but carries associations of the ugly and coarse. The passage is one, therefore,
of many instances of Eliot's device of using something which in one
context is innocent but in another context becomes loaded with a
special meaning.

The Philomela passage has another importance, however. If it is
a commentary on how the waste land became waste, it also repeats
the theme of the death which is the door to life, the theme of the

dying god. The raped woman becomes transformed through suffering into the nightingale; through the violation comes the "inviolable voice." The thesis that suffering is action, and that out of suffering comes poetry is a favorite one of Eliot's. For example, "Shakespeare, too, was occupied with the struggle—which alone constitutes life for a poet—to transmute his personal and private agonies into something rich and strange, something universal and impersonal." Consider also his statement with reference to Baudelaire: "Indeed, in his way of suffering is already a kind of presence of the supernatural and of the superhuman. He rejects always the purely natural and the purely human; in other words, he is neither 'naturalist' nor 'humanist.' " The theme of the life which is death is stated specifically in the conversation between the man and the woman. She asks the question, "Are you alive, or not?" Compare the Dante references in "The Burial of the Dead." (She also asks, "Is there nothing in your head?" He is one of the Hollow Men—"Headpiece filled with straw.") These people, as people living in the waste land, know nothing, see nothing, do not even live.

But the protagonist, after this reflection that in the waste land of modern life even death is sterile—"I think we are in rats' alley/Where the dead men lost their bones"—remembers a death that was transformed into something rich and strange, the death described in the song from *The Tempest*—"Those are pearls that were his eyes."

The reference to this section of *The Tempest* is, like the Philomela reference, one of Eliot's major symbols. A general comment on it is therefore appropriate here, for we are to meet with it twice more in later sections of the poem. The song, one remembers, was sung by Ariel in luring Ferdinand, Prince of Naples, on to meet Miranda, and thus to find love, and through this love, to effect the regeneration and deliverance of all the people on the island. Ferdinand, hearing the song, says:

> The ditty does remember my drowned father.
> This is no mortal business, nor no sound
> That the earth owes . . .

The allusion is an extremely interesting example of the device of Eliot's already commented upon, that of taking an item from one context and shifting it into another in which it assumes a new and powerful meaning. The description of a death which is a portal into a realm of the rich and strange—a death which becomes a sort of birth—assumes in the mind of the protagonist an association with that of the drowned god whose effigy was thrown into the water as a symbol of the death of the fruitful powers of nature but which was taken out of the water as a symbol of the revivified god. (See *From Ritual to Romance.*) The passage therefore represents the perfect antithesis to the passage in "The Burial of the Dead": "That corpse you planted last year in your garden," etc. It also, as we have already pointed out, finds its antithesis in the sterile and unfruitful death "in rats' alley" just commented upon. (We shall find that this contrast between the death in rats' alley and the death in *The Tempest* is made again in "The Fire Sermon.")

We have yet to treat the relation of the title of the second section, "A Game of Chess," to Middleton's play, *Women Beware Women,* from which the game of chess is taken. In the play, the game is used as a device to keep the widow occupied while her daughter-in-law is being seduced. The seduction amounts almost to a rape, and in a *double entendre,* the rape is actually described in terms of the game. We have one more connection with the Philomela symbol, therefore. The abstract game is being used in the contemporary waste land, as in the play, to cover up a rape and is a description of the rape itself.

In the latter part of "A Game of Chess" we are given a picture of spiritual emptiness, but this time, at the other end of the social scale, as reflected in the talk between two cockney women in a London pub. (It is perhaps unnecessary to comment on the relation of their talk about abortion to the theme of sterility and the waste land.)

The account here is straightforward enough, and the only matter which calls for comment is the line spoken by Ophelia in *Hamlet,* which ends the passage. Ophelia, too, was very much concerned about love, the theme of conversation between the women in the pub. As a matter of fact, she was in very much the same position as that of the woman who has been the topic of conversation between the two ladies whom we have just heard. And her poetry, like Philomela's, had come out of suffering. We are probably to look for the relevance of the allusion to her here rather than in an easy satiric contrast between Elizabethan glories and modern sordidness. After all, Eliot's criticism of the present world is not merely the sentimental one that this happens to be the twentieth century after Christ and not the seventeenth.

III

"The Fire Sermon" makes much use of several of the symbols already developed. The fire is the sterile burning of lust, and the section is a sermon, although a sermon by example only. This section of the poem also contains some of the most easily apprehended uses of literary allusion. The poem opens on a vision of the modern river. In Spenser's "Prothalamion" the scene described is also a river scene at London, and it is dominated by nymphs and their paramours, and the nymphs are preparing for a wedding. The contrast between Spenser's scene and its twentieth century equivalent is jarring. The paramours are now "the loitering heirs of city directors," and, as for the nuptials of Spenser's Elizabethan maidens, in the stanzas which follow we learn a great deal about those. At the end of the section the speech of the third of the Thames-nymphs summarizes the whole matter for us.

The waters of the Thames are also associated with those of Leman —the poet in the contemporary waste land is in a sort of Babylonian Captivity.

The castle of the Fisher King was always located on the banks of a river or on the sea shore. The title "Fisher King," Miss Weston shows, originates from the use of the fish as a fertility or life symbol. This meaning, however, was often forgotten, and so his title in many of the later Grail romances is accounted for by describing the king as fishing. Eliot uses the reference to fishing for reverse effect. The reference to fishing is part of the realistic detail of the scene—"While I was fishing in the dull canal." But to the reader who knows the Weston references, the reference is to that of the Fisher King of the Grail legends. The protagonist is the maimed and impotent king of the legends.

Eliot proceeds now to tie the waste-land symbol to that of *The Tempest*, by quoting one of the lines spoken by Ferdinand, Prince of Naples, which occurs just before Ariel's song, "Full Fathom Five," is heard. But he alters *The Tempest* passage somewhat, writing not, "Weeping again the king my father's wreck," but

> Musing upon the king my brother's wreck
> And on the king my father's death before him.

It is possible that the alteration has been made to bring the account taken from *The Tempest* into accord with the situation in the Percival stories. In Wolfram von Eschenbach's *Parzival,* for instance, Trevrezent, the hermit, is the brother of the Fisher King, Anfortas. He tells Parzival, "His name all men know as Anfortas, and I weep for him evermore." Their father, Frimutel, is dead.

The protagonist in the poem, then, imagines himself not only in the situation of Ferdinand in *The Tempest* but also in that of one of the characters in the Grail legend; and the wreck, to be applied literally in the first instance, applies metaphorically in the second.

After the lines from *The Tempest,* appears again the image of a sterile death from which no life comes, the bones, "rattled by the rat's foot only, year to year." (The collocation of this figure with the vision of the death by water in Ariel's song has already been commented on. The lines quoted from *The Tempest* come just before the song.)

The allusion to Marvell's "To His Coy Mistress" is of course one of the easiest allusions in the poem. Instead of "Time's winged chariot" the poet hears "the sound of horns and motors" of contemporary London. But the passage has been further complicated. The reference has been combined with an allusion to Day's "Parliament of Bees." "Time's winged chariot" of Marvell has not only been changed to the modern automobile; Day's "sound of horns and hunting" has changed to the horns of the motors. And Actaeon will not be brought face to face with Diana, goddess of chastity; Sweeney, type of the vulgar bourgeois, is to be brought to Mrs. Porter, hardly a type of chastity. The reference in the ballad to the feet "washed in soda water" reminds the poet ironically of another sort of foot-washing, the sound of the children singing in the dome heard at the ceremony of the foot-washing which precedes the restoration of the wounded Anfortas (the Fisher King) by Parzival and the taking away of the curse from the waste land. The quotation thus completes the allusion to the Fisher King commenced in line 189—"While I was fishing in the dull canal."

The pure song of the children also reminds the poet of the song of the nightingale which we have heard in "The Game of Chess." The recapitulation of symbols is continued with a repetition of "Unreal city" and with the reference to the one-eyed merchant.

Mr. Eugenides, the Smyrna merchant, is the one-eyed merchant mentioned by Madame Sosostris. The fact that the merchant is one-eyed apparently means, in Madame Sosostris' speech, no more than that the merchant's face on the card is shown in profile. But Eliot applies the term to Mr. Eugenides for a totally different effect. The defect corresponds somewhat to Madame Sosostris' bad cold. He is a rather battered representative of the fertility cults: the prophet, the *seer,* with only one eye.

The Syrian merchants, we learn from Miss Weston's book, were, along with slaves and soldiers, the principal carriers of the mysteries which lie at the core of the Grail legends. But in the modern world we find both the representatives of the Tarot divining and the mystery cults in decay. What he carries on his back and what the fortune teller is forbidden to see is evidently the knowledge of the mysteries (although Mr. Eugenides himself is hardly likely to be more aware of it than Madame Sosostris is aware of the importance of her function). Mr. Eugenides, in terms of his former function, ought to be inviting the protagonist into the esoteric cult which holds the secret of life, but on the realistic surface of the poem, in his invitation to "a weekend at the Metropole" he is really inviting him to a homosexual debauch. The homosexuality is "secret" and now a "cult" but a very different cult from that which Mr. Eugenides ought to represent. The end of the new cult is not life but, ironically, sterility.

In the modern waste land, however, even the relation between man and woman is also sterile. The incident between the typist and the carbuncular young man is a picture of "love" so exclusively and practically pursued that it is not love at all. The tragic chorus to the scene is Tiresias, into whom perhaps Mr. Eugenides may be said to modulate, Tiresias, the historical "expert" on the relation between the sexes.

The fact that Tiresias is made the commentator serves a further irony. In *Oedipus Rex,* it is Tiresias who recognizes that the curse which has come upon the Theban land has been caused by the sinful sexual relationship of Oedipus and Jocasta. But Oedipus' sin has been committed in ignorance, and knowledge of it brings horror and remorse. The essential horror of the act which Tiresias witnesses in the poem is that it is not regarded as a sin at all—is perfectly casual, is merely the copulation of beasts.

The reminiscence of the lines from Goldsmith's song in the description of the young woman's actions after the departure of her lover, gives concretely and ironically the utter breakdown of traditional standards.

It is the music of her gramophone which the protagonist hears "creep by" him "on the waters." Far from the music which Ferdinand heard bringing him to Miranda and love, it is, one is tempted to think, the music of "O O O O that Shakespeherian Rag."

But the protagonist says that he can *sometimes* hear "the pleasant whining of a mandoline." Significantly enough, it is the music of the fishmen (the fish again as a life symbol) and it comes from beside a church (though—if this is not to rely too much on Eliot's note—the church has been marked for destruction). Life on Lower Thames Street, if not on the Strand, still has meaning as it cannot have meaning for either the typist or the rich woman of "A Game of Chess."

The song of the Thames-daughters brings us back to the opening section of "The Fire Sermon" again, and once more we have to do with the river and the river-nymphs. Indeed, the typist incident is framed by the two river-nymph scenes.

The connection of the river-nymphs with the Rhine-daughters of Wagner's *Götterdämmerung* is easily made. In the passage in Wagner's opera (to which Eliot refers in his note), the opening of Act III, the Rhine-daughters bewail the loss of the beauty of the Rhine occasioned by the theft of the gold, and then beg Siegfried to give them back the Ring made from this gold, finally threatening him with death if he does not give it up. Like the Thames-daughters they too have been violated; and like the maidens mentioned in the Grail legend, the violation has brought a curse on gods and men. The first of the songs depicts the modern river, soiled with oil and tar. (Compare also with the description of the river in the first part of "The Fire Sermon.") The second song depicts the Elizabethan river, also evoked in the first part of "The Fire Sermon." (Leicester and Elizabeth ride upon it in a barge of state. Incidentally, Spenser's "Prothalamion" from which quotation is made in the first part of "The Fire Sermon" mentions Leicester as having formerly lived in the house which forms the setting of the poem.)

In this second song there is also a definite allusion to the passage in *Antony and Cleopatra* already referred to in the opening line of "A Game of Chess."

> Beating oars
> The stern was formed
> A gilded shell

And if we still have any doubt of the allusion, Eliot's note on the passage with its reference to the "barge" and "poop" should settle the matter. We have already commented on the earlier allusion to Cleopatra as the prime example of love for love's sake. The symbol bears something of the same meaning here, and the note which Eliot supplies does something to reinforce the "Cleopatra" aspect of Elizabeth. Elizabeth in the presence of the Spaniard De Quadra, though negotiations were going on for a Spanish marriage, "went so far that Lord Robert at last said, as I [De Quadra was a bishop] was on the spot there was no reason why they should not be married if the queen pleased." The passage has a sort of double function. It reinforces the general contrast between Elizabethan magnificence and modern sordidness: in the Elizabethan age love for love's sake has some meaning and therefore some magnificence. But the passage gives something of an opposed effect too: the same sterile love, emptiness of love, obtained in this period too: Elizabeth and the typist are alike as well as different. (One of the reasons for the frequent allusion to Elizabethan poetry in this and the preceding section of the poem may be the fact that with the English Renaissance the old set of supernatural sanctions had begun to break up. See Eliot's various essays on Shakespeare and the Elizabethan dramatists.)

The third Thames-daughter's song depicts another sordid "love" affair, and unites the themes of the first two songs. It begins "Trams and *dusty* trees." With it we are definitely in the waste land again. Pia, whose words she echoes in saying "Highbury bore me. Richmond and Kew/Undid me" was in Purgatory and had hope. The woman speaking here has no hope—she too is in the Inferno: "I can connect/ Nothing with nothing." She has just completed, floating down the river in the canoe, what Eliot has described in *Murder in the Cathedral* as

> . . . the effortless journey, to the empty land
>
> .   .   .   .
>
> Where those who were men can no longer turn the mind
> To distraction, delusion, escape into dream, pretence,
> Where the soul is no longer deceived, for there are no objects, no tones,
> No colours, no forms to distract, to divert the soul
> From seeing itself, foully united forever, nothing with nothing,
> Not what we call death, but what beyond death is not death . . .

Now, "on Margate Sands," like the Hollow Men, she stands "on this beach of the tumid river."

The songs of the three Thames-daughters, as a matter of fact, epitomize this whole section of the poem. With reference to the quotations from St. Augustine and Buddha at the end of "The Fire Sermon" Eliot states that "the collocation of these two representatives of eastern and western asceticism, as the culmination of this part of the poem, is not an accident."

It is certainly not an accident. The moral of all the incidents which we have been witnessing is that there must be an asceticism—something to check the drive of desire. The wisdom of the East and the West comes to the same thing on this point. Moreover, the imagery which both St. Augustine and Buddha use for lust is fire. What we have witnessed in the various scenes of "The Fire Sermon" is the sterile burning of lust. Modern man, freed from all restraints, in his cultivation of experience for experience's sake burns, but not with a "hard, gemlike flame." One ought not to pound the point home in this fashion, but to see that the imagery of this section of the poem furnishes illustrations leading up to the Fire Sermon is the necessary

requirement for feeling the force of the brief allusions here at the
end to Buddha and St. Augustine.

IV

Whatever the specific meaning of the symbols, the general function
of the section, "Death by Water," is readily apparent. The section
forms a contrast with "The Fire Sermon" which precedes it—a contrast between the symbolism of fire and that of water. Also readily
apparent is its force as a symbol of surrender and relief through surrender.

Some specific connections can be made, however. The drowned
Phoenician Sailor recalls the drowned god of the fertility cults. Miss
Weston tells that each year at Alexandria an effigy of the head of the
god was thrown into the water as a symbol of the death of the powers
of nature, and that this head was carried by the current to Byblos
where it was taken out of the water and exhibited as a symbol of the
reborn god.

Moreover, the Phoenician Sailor is a merchant—"Forgot . . . the
profit and loss." The vision of the drowned sailor gives a statement
of the message which the Syrian merchants originally brought to
Britain and which the Smyrna merchant, unconsciously and by ironical negatives, has brought. One of Eliot's notes states that the "merchant . . . melts into the Phoenician Sailor, and the latter is not
wholly distinct from Ferdinand Prince of Naples." The death by
water would seem to be equated with the death described in Ariel's
song in *The Tempest*. There is a definite difference in the tone of
the description of this death—"A current under sea/Picked his bones
in whispers," as compared with the "other" death—"bones cast in a
little low dry garret,/Rattled by the rat's foot only, year to year."

Further than this it would not be safe to go, but one may point out
that whirling (the whirlpool here, the Wheel of Madame Sosostris'
palaver) is one of Eliot's symbols frequently used in other poems
(*Ash Wednesday*, "Gerontion," *Murder in the Cathedral,* and "Burnt
Norton") to denote the temporal world. And I may point out, supplying the italics myself, the following passage from *Ash Wednesday:*

> Although I do not hope to *turn* again
>
> .   .   .   .
>
> Wavering between the *profit and the loss*
> In this brief transit where the dreams cross
> The dreamcrossed twilight *between birth and dying.*

At least, with a kind of hindsight, one may suggest that "Death by

Water" gives an instance of the conquest of death and time, the "perpetual recurrence of determined seasons," the "world of spring and autumn, birth and dying" through death itself.

V

The reference to the "torchlight red on sweaty faces" and to the "frosty silence in the gardens" obviously associates Christ in Gethsemane with the other hanged gods. The god has now died, and in referring to this, the basic theme finds another strong restatement:

> He who was living is now dead
> We who were living are now dying
> With a little patience

The poet does not say "We who *are* living." It is "We who *were* living." It is the death-in-life of Dante's Limbo. Life in the full sense has been lost.

The passage on the sterility of the waste land and the lack of water provides for the introduction later of two highly important passages:

> There is not even silence in the mountains
> But dry sterile thunder without rain

—lines which look forward to the introduction later of "what the thunder said" when the thunder, no longer sterile, but bringing rain, speaks.

The second of these passages is, "There is not even solitude in the mountains," which looks forward to the reference to the Journey to Emmaus theme a few lines later: "Who is the third who walks always beside you?" The god has returned, has arisen, but the travelers cannot tell whether it is really he, or mere illusion induced by their delirium.

The parallelism between the "hooded figure" who "walks always beside you" and the "hooded hordes" is another instance of the sort of parallelism that is really a contrast. In the first case, the figure is indistinct because spiritual; in the second, the hooded hordes are indistinct because completely *unspiritual*—they are the people of the waste land—

> Shape without form, shade without colour,
> Paralysed force, gesture without motion

—to take two lines from "The Hollow Men," where the people of the waste land once more appear. Or to take another line from the same poem, perhaps their hoods are the "deliberate disguises" which the Hollow Men, the people of the waste land, wear.

Eliot, as his notes tell us, has particularly connected the description here with the "decay of eastern Europe." The hordes represent, then, the general waste land of the modern world with a special application to the breakup of Eastern Europe, the region with which the fertility cults were especially connected and in which today the traditional values are thoroughly discredited. The cities, Jerusalem, Athens, Alexandria, Vienna, like the London of the first section of the poem are "unreal," and for the same reason.

The passage which immediately follows develops the unreality into nightmare, but it is a nightmare vision which is something more than an extension of the passage beginning, "What is the city over the mountains"—in it appear other figures from earlier in the poem: the lady of "A Game of Chess," who, surrounded by the glory of history and art, sees no meaning in either and threatens to rush out into the street "With my hair down, so," has here let down her hair and fiddles "whisper music on those strings." One remembers in "A Game of Chess" that it was the woman's hair that spoke:

> . . . her hair
> Spread out in fiery points
> Glowed into words, then would be savagely still.

The hair has been immemorially a symbol of fertility, and Miss Weston and Frazer mention sacrifices of hair in order to aid the fertility god.

As we have pointed out earlier, this passage is also to be connected with the twelfth chapter of Ecclesiastes. The doors "of mudcracked houses," and the cisterns in this passage are to be found in Ecclesiastes, and the woman fiddling music from her hair is one of "the daughters of music" brought low. The towers and bells from the Elizabeth and Leicester passage of "The Fire Sermon" also appear here, but the towers are upside down, and the bells, far from pealing for an actual occasion or ringing the hours, are "reminiscent." The civilization is breaking up.

The "violet light" also deserves comment. In "The Fire Sermon" it is twice mentioned as the "violet hour," and there it has little more than a physical meaning. It is a description of the hour of twilight. Here it indicates the twilight of the civilization, but it is perhaps something more. Violet is one of the liturgical colors of the Church. It symbolizes repentance and it is the color of baptism. The visit to the Perilous Chapel, according to Miss Weston, was an initiation— that is, a baptism. In the nightmare vision, the bats wear baby faces.

The horror built up in this passage is a proper preparation for the passage on the Perilous Chapel which follows it. The journey has not been merely an agonized walk in the desert, though it is that; nor is it merely the journey after the god has died and hope has been lost; it is also the journey to the Perilous Chapel of the Grail story. In Miss Weston's account, the Chapel was part of the ritual, and was filled with horrors to test the candidate's courage. In some stories the perilous cemetery is also mentioned. Eliot has used both: "Over the tumbled graves, about the chapel." In many of the Grail stories the Chapel was haunted by demons.

The cock in the folklore of many people is regarded as the bird whose voice chases away the powers of evil. It is significant that it is after his crow that the flash of lightning comes and the "damp gust/ Bringing rain." It is just possible that the cock has a connection also with *The Tempest* symbols. The first song which Ariel sings to Ferdinand as he sits "Weeping again the king my father's wreck" ends

> The strain of strutting chanticleer,
> Cry, cock-a-doodle-doo.

The next stanza is the "Full Fathom Five" song which Eliot has used as a vision of life gained through death. If this relation holds, here we have an extreme instance of an allusion, in itself innocent, forced into serious meaning through transference to a new context.

As Miss Weston has shown, the fertility cults go back to a very early period and are recorded in Sanscrit legends. Eliot has been continually, in the poem, linking up the Christian doctrine with the beliefs of as many peoples as he can. Here he goes back to the very beginnings of Aryan culture, and tells the rest of the story of the rain's coming, not in terms of the setting already developed but in its earliest form. The passage is thus a perfect parallel in method to the passage in "The Burial of the Dead":

> "You who were with me in the ships *at Mylae!*
> "That corpse you planted *last year* in your garden . . ."

The use of Sanscrit in what the thunder says is thus accounted for. In addition, there is of course a more obvious reason for casting what the thunder said into Sanscrit here: onomatopoeia.

The comments on the three statements of the thunder imply an acceptance of them. The protagonist answers the first question, "What have we given? with the statement:

> The awful daring of a moment's surrender
> Which an age of prudence can never retract
> By this, and this only, we have existed.

Here the larger meaning is stated in terms which imply the sexual meaning. Man cannot be absolutely self-regarding. Even the propagation of the race—even mere "existence"—calls for such a surrender. Living calls for—see the passage already quoted from Eliot's essay on Baudelaire—belief in something more than "life."

The comment on *dayadhvam* (sympathize) is obviously connected with the foregoing passage. The surrender to something outside the self is an attempt (whether on the sexual level or some other) to transcend one's essential isolation. The passage gathers up the symbols previously developed in the poem just as the foregoing passage reflects, though with a different implication, the numerous references to sex made earlier in the poem. For example, the woman in the first part of "A Game of Chess" has also heard the key turn in the door, and confirms her prison by thinking of the key:

> "Speak to me. Why do you never speak. Speak.
> "What are you thinking of? What thinking? What?
> "I never know what you are thinking. Think."

The third statement made by the thunder, *damyata* (control), follows the condition necessary for control, sympathy. The figure of the boat catches up the figure of control already given in "Death by Water"—"O you who turn the wheel and look to windward"—and from "The Burial of the Dead" the figure of happy love in which the ship rushes on with a fair wind behind it: *"Frisch weht der Wind . . ."*

I cannot accept Mr. Leavis' interpretation of the passage, "I sat upon the shore/Fishing, with the arid plain behind me," as meaning that the poem "exhibits no progression." The comment upon what the thunder says would indicate, if other passages did not, that the poem does "not end where it began." It is true that the protagonist does not witness a revival of the waste land; but there are two important relationships involved in his case: a personal one as well as a general one. If secularization has destroyed, or is likely to destroy, modern civilization, the protagonist still has a private obligation to fulfill. Even if the civilization is breaking up—"London Bridge is falling down falling down falling down"—there remains the personal obligation: "Shall I at least set my lands in order?" Consider in this connection the last sentences of Eliot's "Thoughts After Lambeth": "The World is trying the experiment of attempting to form a civilized but non-Christian mentality. The experiment will fail; but we must be very patient in awaiting its collapse; meanwhile redeeming the time: so that the Faith may be preserved alive through the dark ages before us; to renew and rebuild civilization, and save the World from suicide."

The bundle of quotations with which the poem ends has a very definite relation to the general theme of the poem and to several of the major symbols used in the poem. Before Arnaut leaps back into the refining fire of Purgatory with joy he says: "I am Arnaut who weep and go singing; contrite I see my past folly, and joyful I see before me the day I hope for. Now I pray you by that virtue which guides you to the summit of the stair, at times be mindful of my pain." This theme is carried forward by the quotation from *Pervigilium Veneris:* "When shall I be like the swallow." The allusion is also connected with the Philomela symbol. (Eliot's note on the passage indicates this clearly.) The sister of Philomela was changed into a swallow as Philomela was changed into a nightingale. The protagonist is asking therefore when shall the spring, the time of love, return, but also when will he be reborn out of his sufferings, and—with the special meaning which the symbol takes on from the preceding Dante quotation and from the earlier contexts already discussed—he is asking what is asked at the end of one of the minor poems: "When will Time flow away."

The quotation from "El Desdichado," as Edmund Wilson has pointed out, indicates that the protagonist of the poem has been disinherited, robbed of his tradition. The ruined tower is perhaps also the Perilous Chapel, "only the wind's home," and it is also the whole tradition in decay. The protagonist resolves to claim his tradition and rehabilitate it.

The quotation from *The Spanish Tragedy*—"Why then Ile fit you. Hieronymo's mad againe"—is perhaps the most puzzling of all these quotations. It means, I believe, this: The protagonist's acceptance of what is in reality the deepest truth will seem to the present world mere madness. ("And still she cried . . . 'Jug Jug' to dirty ears.") Hieronymo in the play, like Hamlet, was "mad" for a purpose. The protagonist is conscious of the interpretation which will be placed on the words which follow—words which will seem to many apparently meaningless babble, but which contain the oldest and most permanent truth of the race:

Datta. Dayadhvam. Damyata.

Quotation of the whole context from which the line is taken confirms this interpretation. Hieronymo, asked to write a play for the court's entertainment, replies:

Why then, I'll fit you; say no more.
When I was young, I gave my mind
And plied myself to fruitless poetry;

> Which though it profit the professor naught,
> Yet it is passing pleasing to the world.

He sees that the play will give him the opportunity he has been seeking to avenge his son's murder. Like Hieronymo, the protagonist in the poem has found his theme; what he is about to perform is not "fruitless."

After this repetition of what the thunder said comes the benediction:

> Shantih   shantih   shantih

The foregoing account of *The Waste Land* is, of course, not to be substituted for the poem itself. Moreover, it certainly is not to be considered as representing *the method by which the poem was composed.* Much which the prose expositor must represent as though it had been consciously contrived obviously was arrived at unconsciously and concretely.

The account given above is a statement merely of the "prose meaning," and bears the same relation to the poem as does the "prose meaning" of any other poem. But one need not perhaps apologize for setting forth such a statement explicitly, for *The Waste Land* has been almost consistently misinterpreted since its first publication. Even a critic so acute as Edmund Wilson has seen the poem as essentially a statement of despair and disillusionment, and his account sums up the stock interpretation of the poem. Indeed, the phrase, "the poetry of drouth," has become a cliché of left-wing criticism. It is such a misrepresentation of *The Waste Land* as this which allows Eda Lou Walton to entitle an essay on contemporary poetry, "Death in the Desert"; or which causes Waldo Frank to misconceive of Eliot's whole position and personality. But more than the meaning of one poem is at stake. If *The Waste Land* is not a world-weary cry of despair or a sighing after the vanished glories of the past, then not only the popular interpretation of the poem will have to be altered but also the general interpretations of postwar poetry which begin with such a misinterpretation as a premise.

Such misinterpretations involve also misconceptions of Eliot's technique. Eliot's basic method may be said to have passed relatively unnoticed. The popular view of the method used in *The Waste Land* may be described as follows: Eliot makes use of ironic contrasts between the glorious past and the sordid present—the crashing irony of

> But at my back from time to time I hear
> The sound of horns and motors, which shall bring
> Sweeney to Mrs. Porter in the spring.

But this is to take the irony of the poem at the most superficial level, and to neglect the other dimensions in which it operates. And it is to neglect what are essentially more important aspects of his method. Moreover, it is to overemphasize the difference between the method employed by Eliot in this poem and that employed by him in later poems.

The basic method used in *The Waste Land* may be described as the application of the principle of complexity. The poet works in terms of surface parallelisms which in reality make ironical contrasts, and in terms of surface contrasts which in reality constitute parallelisms. (The second group sets up effects which may be described as the obverse of irony.) The two aspects taken together give the effect of chaotic experience ordered into a new whole, though the realistic surface of experience is faithfully retained. The complexity of the experience is not violated by the apparent forcing upon it of a predetermined scheme.

The fortune telling of "The Burial of the Dead" will illustrate the general method very satisfactorily. On the surface of the poem the poet reproduces the patter of the charlatan, Madame Sosostris, and there is the surface irony: the contrast between the original use of the Tarot cards and the use made by Madame Sosostris. But each of the details (justified realistically in the palaver of the fortune teller) assumes a new meaning in the general context of the poem. There is then, in addition to the surface irony, something of a Sophoclean irony too, and the "fortune telling," which is taken ironically by a twentieth century audience, becomes *true* as the poem develops—true in a sense in which Madame Sosostris herself does not think it true. The surface irony is thus reversed and becomes an irony on a deeper level. The items of her speech have only one reference in terms of the context of her speech: the "man with three staves," the "one-eyed merchant," the "crowds of people, walking round in a ring," etc. But transferred to other contexts they become loaded with special meanings. To sum up, all the central symbols of the poem head up here; but here, in the only section in which they are explicitly bound together, the binding is slight and accidental. The deeper lines of association only emerge in terms of the total context as the poem develops—and this is, of course, exactly the effect which the poet intends.

This transference of items from an "innocent" context into a context in which they become charged and transformed in meaning will account for many of the literary allusions in the poem. For example, the "change of Philomel" is merely one of the items in the decorative detail in the room in the opening of "A Game of Chess." But the violent change of tense—"And still she cried, and still the world pursues"

—makes it a comment upon, and a symbol of, the modern world. And further allusions to it through the course of the poem gradually equate it with the general theme of the poem. The allusions to *The Tempest* display the same method. The parallelism between Dante's Hell and the waste land of the Grail legends is fairly close; even the equation of Baudelaire's Paris to the waste land is fairly obvious. But the parallelism between the death by drowning in *The Tempest* and the death of the fertility god is, on the surface, merely accidental, and the first allusion to Ariel's song is merely an irrelevant and random association of the stream-of-consciousness:

> Is your card, the drowned Phoenician Sailor,
> (Those are pearls that were his eyes. Look!)

And on its second appearance in "A Game of Chess" it is still only an item in the protagonist's abstracted reverie. Even the association of *The Tempest* symbol with the Grail legends in the lines

> While I was fishing in the dull canal
> .   .   .   .
> Musing upon the king my brother's wreck

and in the passage which follows, is ironical merely. But the associations have been established, even though they may seem to be made in ironic mockery, and when we come to the passage, "Death by Water," with its change of tone, they assert themselves positively. We have a sense of revelation out of material apparently accidentally thrown together. I have called the effect the obverse of irony, for the method, like that of irony, is indirect, though the effect is positive rather than negative.

The melting of the characters into each other is, of course, an aspect of this general process. Elizabeth and the girl born at Highbury both ride on the Thames, one in the barge of state, the other supine in a narrow canoe, and they are both Thames-nymphs, who are violated and thus are like the Rhine-nymphs who have also been violated, etc. With the characters as with the other symbols, the surface relationships may be accidental and apparently trivial and they may be made either ironically or through random association or in hallucination, but in the total context of the poem the deeper relationships are revealed. The effect is a sense of the oneness of experience, and of the unity of all periods, and with this, a sense that the general theme of the poem is true. But the theme has not been imposed—it has been revealed.

This complication of parallelisms and contrasts makes, of course, for ambiguity, but the ambiguity, in part, resides in the poet's fidelity to the complexity of experience. The symbols resist complete equation with a simple meaning. To take an example, "rock" throughout the poem seems to be one of the "desert" symbols. For example, the "dry stone" gives "no sound of water"; woman in the waste land is "the Lady of the Rocks," and most pointed of all, there is the long delirium passage in "What the Thunder Said": "Here is no water but only rock," etc. So much for its general meaning, but in "The Burial of the Dead" occur the lines

> Only
> There is shadow under this red rock,
> (Come in under the shadow of this red rock).

Rock here is a place of refuge. (Moreover, there may also be a reference to the Grail symbolism. In *Parzival,* the Grail is a stone: "And this stone all men call the grail . . . As children the Grail doth call them, 'neath its shadow they wax and grow.") The paradox, life through death, penetrates the symbol itself.

To take an even clearer case of this paradoxical use of symbols, consider the lines which occur in the hyacinth girl passage. The vision gives obviously a sense of the richness and beauty of life. It is a moment of ecstasy (the basic imagery is obviously sexual); but the moment in its intensity is like death. The protagonist looks in that moment into the "heart of light, the silence," and so looks into—not richness—but blankness: he is neither "living nor dead." The symbol of life stands also for a kind of death. This duality of function may, of course, extend to a whole passage. For example, consider:

> Where fishmen lounge at noon: where the walls
> Of Magnus Martyr hold
> Inexplicable splendour of Ionian white and gold.

The function of the passage is to indicate the poverty into which religion has fallen: the splendid church now surrounded by the poorer districts. But the passage has an opposed effect also: the fishmen in the "public bar in Lower Thames Street" next to the church have a meaningful life which has been largely lost to the secularized upper and middle classes.

The poem would undoubtedly be "clearer" if every symbol had a single, unequivocal meaning; but the poem would be thinner, and less honest. For the poet has not been content to develop a didactic allegory in which the symbols are two-dimensional items adding up directly to the sum of the general scheme. They represent dramatized

instances of the theme, embodying in their own nature the funda-
mental paradox of the theme.

We shall better understand why the form of the poem is right and
inevitable if we compare Eliot's theme to Dante's and to Spenser's.
Eliot's theme is not the statement of a faith held and agreed upon
(Dante's *Divine Comedy*) nor is it the projection of a "new" system
of beliefs (Spenser's *Faerie Queene*). Eliot's theme is the rehabilitation of a system of beliefs, known but now discredited. Dante did not
have to "prove" his statement; he could assume it and move within
it about a poet's business. Eliot does not care, like Spenser, to force
the didacticism. He prefers to stick to the poet's business. But, unlike
Dante, he cannot assume acceptance of the statement. A direct approach is calculated to elicit powerful "stock responses" which will
prevent the poem's being *read* at all. Consequently, the only method
is to work by indirection. The Christian material is at the center, but
the poet never deals with it directly. The theme of resurrection is
made on the surface in terms of the fertility rites; the words which
the thunder speaks are Sanscrit words.

We have been speaking as if the poet were a strategist trying to
win acceptance from a hostile audience. But of course this is true only
in a sense. The poet himself is audience as well as speaker; we state
the problem more exactly if we state it in terms of the poet's integrity
rather than in terms of his strategy. He is so much a man of his own
age that he can indicate his attitude toward the Christian tradition
without falsity only in terms of the difficulties of a rehabilitation; and
he is so much a poet and so little a propagandist that he can be sin-
cere only as he presents his theme concretely and dramatically.

To put the matter in still other terms: the Christian terminology
is for the poet a mass of clichés. However "true" he may feel the
terms to be, he is still sensitive to the fact that they operate superficially as clichés, and his method of necessity must be a process of
bringing them to life again. The method adopted in *The Waste
Land* is thus violent and radical, but thoroughly necessary. For the
renewing and vitalizing of symbols which have been crusted over with
a distorting familiarity demands the type of organization which we
have already commented on in discussing particular passages: the
statement of surface similarities which are ironically revealed to be
dissimilarities, and the association of apparently obvious dissimilarities which culminates in a later realization that the dissimilarities
are only superficial—that the chains of likeness are in reality funda-
mental. In this way the statement of beliefs emerges *through* confusion and cynicism—not in spite of them.

Modern Art Techniques in *The Waste Land*

by Jacob Korg

Le beau est toujours bizarre.
—BAUDELAIRE

Because *The Waste Land* is securely established as one of the most significant poems of the twentieth century, we are in danger of forgetting that it is, by any standard, an extremely eccentric work. Many of its peculiarities have been attributed to the various influences operating upon Eliot, and to the spirit of protest against nineteenth century conventions characteristic of the art of the early twentieth century, but explanations of this sort do not do justice to the poem's Promethean originality. Critics seeking illuminating analogies from the other arts for the anomalous construction of *The Waste Land* have turned most often to music; the poem has been compared to a Beethoven symphony and other musical forms, and its method has been termed a "music of ideas." However, if Eliot's departures from traditional poetic methods are considered, not merely as indications of influence or rebellion, but as expressive resources which suited his intentions and corresponded to his feelings, another parallel suggests itself. The sensibility displayed by *The Waste Land's* stylistic innovations resembles that which animated the technical experiments of the Cubists, Futurists, Dadaists and Surrealists, Eliot's contemporaries in the graphic arts. Each of these movements had its literary aspect, but it is, curiously enough, in the paintings, which in most cases proved to be the most successful results of their experiments, that the closest analogies to the methods of *The Waste Land* are to be found.

The Waste Land is generally described as a collection of fragments. The five sections into which it is divided do not claim to be complete in themselves; further, each of these contains passages which abut upon each other without transitions, and within these appear even smaller units, sometimes single words or phrases, that are incomplete in form and apparently unrelated to their contexts. But, as Edmund

Jacob Korg, "Modern Art Techniques in The Waste Land," *Journal of Aesthetics and Art Criticism, XVIII (June 1960), 456–63. Copyright © 1960 by* The Journal of Aesthetics and Art Criticism. *Reprinted by permission of the author and publisher.*

Wilson, Cleanth Brooks, and other critics have shown, every part of it is connected with the others, not in a conventional way, but by means of a complicated system of echoes, contrasts, parallels, and allusions. The lines from Wagner's *Tristan* in the first section for example, are formless scraps that retain little of the quality of the work from which they are drawn, but they do support the themes of loss and love in the poem as a whole. The dominant figures of the Grail Knight, the Fisher King, and Tiresias, all taken from well-developed traditions of their own, appear only sporadically. The two women in "A Game of Chess" have no actual connection with each other, but the poem relates them within its own design as two contrasting illustrations of the failure of love in modern society. Their stories, as they stand, are incomplete; yet in the context of the poem they form a completion larger than themselves.

This effect, which appears to be the result of an energetic shattering of the subject matter, and a rearrangement of its parts in a markedly different order, will strike anyone who has seen the Cubist paintings of Braque or Picasso or the Futurist works of Severini or Boccioni as familiar. In an effort to see their models as a whole, and to transcend the conventional limitations of perception, the original Cubists, working in a mode which Guillaume Apollinaire called "analytic Cubism," dissected their subjects, cutting them into parts and reassembling them within the picture in new patterns, exactly as a biologist might dissect a frog and lay its organs on his tray in some convenient order. They interpreted space as a series of overlapping planes lying at intervals behind the level of the canvas, through which the objects in the painting move in eccentric patterns. As we examine a Cubist painting, we find that there is no one place where a figure is drawn fully, but that details of its shape are scattered and repeated like a Wagnerian leitmotif. Instead of limiting himself to one angle of vision, the Cubist painter circles around his model, showing the same guitar or bottle of sherry from many different aspects, placing all of these shapes side by side on the same surface, and ordering them into a single design. Or he portrays a head by showing one part of it in profile, the other in full-face, uniting these into a single grotesque form that seems to bend three-dimensional space to the single plane of the canvas.

The Futurist painters, though operating on somewhat different principles, produced results closely allied to the work of the Cubists. They sought to convey powerful emotions, usually tension or anguish, by analyzing the model into suitable design elements, and even by introducing nonrepresentational lines, called *lignes-forces* that run through the paintings. They also used the device of depicting successive states of the model as though they were simultaneous, so that a Futurist painting, like a Cubist one, repeats forms rhythmically in its design. The fragments of the model in a Cubist or Futurist picture do not merely add up to the original; instead, they combine in a new way to form the design of the picture, just as the fragmentary scenes, figures, and allusions of *The Waste Land* send echoes among themselves that relate to the central meaning of the poem.

The fragmentation and reintegration observable in *The Waste Land* can be regarded as the same process as that used by the Cubists and Futurists, springing from a similar intention, and having a comparable effect. *The Waste Land* sees history as a spiritual epic. Using its theme of the decline and renewal of faith as its center of relevance, it successfully combines fragments from the myth of Tiresias, the Grail Legend, the theories of J. G. Frazer and Jessie L. Weston, the Upanishads, and many other sources, both fictional and historical. In presenting such different personages as Tiresias, St. Augustine, and the young man carbuncular as characters in a single drama, Eliot diminishes—though he does not eliminate—our sense of their separation. The process, an exercise in the unification of sensibility, consists of seeing the theme of the poem reflected in widely scattered instances, and using these to give a fuller sense of it than could be drawn from any single subject, no matter how exhaustively it might be treated. It creates that sense of circling about the model and seeing it from many different points of view that is characteristic of analytic Cubism. Eliot seems to be describing a method that would produce these results when he speaks of the poet's mind as

> . . . a receptacle for seizing and storing up numberless feelings, phrases and images, which remain there until all the particles which can unite to form a new compound are present together.[1]

A process which parallels Baudelaire's account of the working of the artistic imagination:

> It decomposes all of creation, and, with the materials gathered, set forth according to rules whose origin cannot be found except in the deepest part of the soul, it creates a new world, and produces the experience of the new.[2]

Eliot's way of presenting history as a series of moments in which such figures as Tiresias, the Fisher King and Mr. Eugenides, or Cleo-

---

[1] "Tradition and the Individual Talent," *Selected Essays* (New York, 1932), p. 8.
[2] Translated from "La reine des facultés," *Salon de 1859.*

patra, Elizabeth, and the unnamed woman in the canoe are caught in comparable poses is strikingly similar to the Cubist method of painting space as a series of planes on which the elements of the design are repeated. Spiritual situations seem to wheel through time in Eliot's poem, much as the forms in a Cubist painting seem to wheel through space. In the Cubist painting, the laws of space are suppressed, so that all parts of the model, even those that are normally out of sight, can be brought actively into the design; similarly, in *The Waste Land*, the laws of time are suppressed so that all of history and literature can be made available to the poem. In short, *The Waste Land* reconstitutes time in much the same way as the Cubist painting reconstitutes space.

We shall not be pressing the analogy between Cubist painting and *The Waste Land* too far if we seek a resemblance in the way the fragments of reality are brought together into a new unity. We have already mentioned one way in which this unity is achieved—the repetition of forms in the painting and themes in the poem. But more powerful integrating forces are at work in both cases, and they operate in ways that parallel each other curiously. Many of the paintings that belong to the early period of Cubism present the appearance of a jungle of lines and shapes, all, according to the principles of analytic Cubism, derived from the model. Yet the model itself is nearly invisible, and is discernible only as a multilated, shadowy shape partly occluded by and partly made up of these fragments of itself. *The Waste Land* presents a similar situation. Its "model," the fable of the loss of faith in the recent history of mankind, is a background presence that dominates the poem. Yet the parallels, counterparts, specific instances, and historical allusions that implement the expression of the central idea seem also to come between the subject and the reader, to smother it beneath a swarm of apparent irrelevancies. In order to understand painting or poem, the observer must first recognize in its shadowy subject an identity familiar in his own experience; he must then trace the means by which the subject has been translated into the idiom of the painting or the poem. Understanding works of this kind means seeing the relationship between the *donnée* and the work of art itself, grasping the forces that have transformed the one into the other. This appreciative process is very different from the one appropriate to more conventional art, in which the main stress is likely to lie upon mere recognition of the artist's success in imitation.

One of the most interesting of *The Waste Land's* innovations is the use of quotations from other poems, songs, and devotional books as a regular rhetorical device. Though Ezra Pound had employed frequent quotations in his sequence, *Hugh Selwyn Mauberley*, Eliot's method differs sufficiently from this and other earlier uses to rank as a genuine departure. Pound's use of quotations in *Mauberley* is essentially like the practice of citing Shakespeare or the Bible in ordinary expository prose; the quotation is a comment supporting its context, and it is something woven cleverly into the syntax of the sentence. For example, in the lines

> Unaffected by the "march of events,"
> He passed from men's memory in *l'an trentiesme*
> *De son eage . . .*

Both the newspaper cliché and the slightly altered quotation from François Villon's *Grand Testament* are assimilated into the sentence, not, it is true, without bringing from their origins a considerable enrichment of meaning. In *The Waste Land,* however, many of the quotations have no syntactical function, and only an oblique relation to their context. The line from Verlaine's *Parsifal* inserted into the song about Mrs. Porter and her daughter, and the line from Kyd's *Spanish Tragedy* near the end of the poem are examples of this technique. These quotations communicate, not by carefully controlled meaning, as the other words in the poem do, but by their associations, which are at once more immediate and less exact than the meanings of words. Their function in the poem resembles that of the passages of dialogue which appear in "The Burial of the Dead" and "A Game of Chess." They exemplify, or embody, meaning. They are realistic exhibits which illustrate directly instead of discussing. They have the irreducible, opaque solidity of *tranches de vie,* communicating on a different level from that of Eliot's own words, and illuminating his meaning from a different direction. In short, they function as objects rather than words, intruding like nonsymbolic foreign matter into the texture of the poem.

When they are approached from this point of view, the unassimilated quotations and realistic conversations of *The Waste Land* are seen to be counterparts of a new technique invented by Braque and Picasso which not only violated the traditional rules of their art, but also seemed to conflict with the essential spirit of Cubist painting. At a time when their work was growing less and less representational, Braque and Picasso occasionally introduced a meticulously realistic detail in the spirit of *trompe-l'oeil,* and then, following this tendency to its ultimate conclusion, began to fasten actual objects onto the canvas. This is the technique known as *collage,* or *papier collé.* In the midst of a painting consisting of shifting planes and grotesque forms the observer is astonished to see an actual bit of wallpaper, a clipping from a newspaper whose headlines and columns are perfectly readable, a piece of an old envelope, or a group of carefully formed letters or numbers. Often enough these elements seem introduced primarily for their colors, shapes, or textures, but there can be no question that this spirited vaulting over the usual limits of art carries with it an unprecedented effect. Hitherto the realm of art could safely be regarded as separate from actuality, no matter how closely it might be made to resemble it. But when actual bits of our own world take their place in a picture side by side with forms created by a painter, the real object seems to demarcate the limit of the painting, forming what Guillaume Apollinaire called an "inner frame," and impressing the observer with the sharp contrast between the realms of art and actuality, thereby freeing him from the assumptions underlying imitative art. In addition, *collage* seems to show that, while art and actuality are discontinuous, they do have the same degree of reality, and can meet at one point of perception. The familiar-looking strip of newsprint, the painted letter or number which is so patently itself and nothing else, serve as character witnesses for the genuineness of the fanciful forms that surround them. Conversely, the invented parts of the painting demonstrate that the homely bits of actuality they embrace have aesthetic qualities of their own.

A device parallel to *collage* operates in *The Waste Land*. By taking nonsymbolic elements borrowed from real life, such as the quotations from "Mrs. Porter and her daughter" and "London Bridge is falling down," and examples of flat, objective realism like the aimless and trivial reminiscences of the character who identifies herself as "Marie," and the talk of the women in "A Game of Chess," and putting them side by side with imagined people and events, the poem insists upon both the distinction and the relationship between art and actuality. The quoted material and lines of mundane dialogue are concrete instances of the spiritual condition which is the theme of the poem. The effect of this technique is similar to the effect of *collage* in painting. The real and the imagined are made to support each other, the real bringing into the work a powerful and unexpected authenticity, and the imagined serving to control the significance of the real elements by interpreting them.

After World War I the revolutionary energies which had produced Cubism and Futurism found their way into new channels, the most significant of which was perhaps Surrealism, a writer's movement that was taken over early in its career by painters. *The Waste Land* was written and published at the time that a group of Parisian writers who had belonged to the Dada movement were experimenting with automatic writing and preparing to initiate a new movement which would counteract the negativism of the old one. The Surrealists believed that they had found in the image-forming and organizing power of the unconscious a new justification for Baudelaire's doctrine of the supremacy of the imagination in art. Through such methods as automatic writing, the investigation of dreams, and interviews with subjects in a trance, they sought to explore psychic reality. Painters entered the movement gradually. The first Surrealist paintings were examples of automatism; next came illustrations of dream situations, and finally paintings with a wide range of techniques that reflected states of mind or opened new frontiers of feeling by the use of enigmatic images. Surrealism stood for the unleashing of repressed psychic energies and the destruction of established moral values. Though its principles and those of Eliot are in nearly all respects exactly opposed to each other, the fact remains that *The Waste Land* is in some ways an unmistakably Surrealist poem.

What the Surrealists meant by "surréalité," or the *real* reality they considered superior to mere appearance, was a combination of material reality with attitudes originating in dreams, fantasies, and mental disorders. The weird quality of Surrealist art is the result of this mingling of the commonplace and the fantastic, whose purpose is to override the usual limitations of perception by enlisting the powers of the subconscious, and thus to capture a reality more profound than that accessible to the senses. *Surréalité* walks on the two legs of ordinary perception and intuitive perception. *The Waste Land* achieves a similar multiplicity of awareness in a similar fashion. The poem as a whole is a two-layered structure which presents the banalities of modern life side by side with the wealth of dark, suggestive myth explored in *The Golden Bough*. It attempts to see at once what is hidden in the memory of the race and what is obvious in the present; the grotesque mingling of contradictory elements that results recalls the true Surrealist vein. Such paradoxical pairings as those of the Rhine maidens and the littered Thames, of Enobarbus' description of Cleopatra and the conversation of a bored modern couple, generate a characteristically Surrealist irony.

Definitions of Surrealism and Surrealist manifestoes have come and gone, but when we say today that something has a Surrealist quality, we mean nothing more specific than it is at once dreamlike and sharply realistic, eerie and funny, unaccountable, yet impressively significant. The Surrealist effect is like that of an image remembered from a dream; it embodies a profound emotional impression, but its meaning remains elusive. Characteristically this effect is produced by joining incongruous elements in such a way that they produce a perceptible, but indefinable sense of relationship. Giorgio de Chirico's painting, "The Child's Brain," for example, shows a mustachioed and hairy-chested man, naked to the waist, looking down thoughtfully at a book lying before him on a table. Marcel Jean's sculpture, "Specter of the Gardenia," is the head of a girl in black plaster with zippers for eyes, and a collar formed with a coil of film. Effects of this kind are the staple element of Surrealist poetry, and Eliot, who occasionally used such images in his earlier poems, offers further excellent examples in *The Waste Land*. When in "The Burial of the Dead," Stetson is asked

> "That corpse you planted last year in your garden,
> Has it begun to sprout? Will it bloom this year?"

the Surrealist quality speaks for itself. The passage in "What the Thunder Said" that begins

> A woman drew her long black hair out tight
> And fiddled whisper music on those strings. . . .

has precisely the atmosphere of portentous, yet inexplicable dream episodes that the Surrealists succeeded in establishing as their characteristic effect. Both of these passages present the standard Surrealist formula, the welding of unrelated elements into a grotesque and enigmatic unity. The image of Stetson's garden, since it yields a coherent allegorical meaning, has only a surface Surrealism. But the verse paragraph about the black-haired woman, with its bats with baby faces, inverted towers, and voices singing out of empty wells, seems terrifyingly meaningful, yet eludes final interpretation, thus achieving the true, disquieting Surrealist quality.

One of the ways in which the Surrealist painters achieved an effect of ambiguity was the double image, the visual pun which enables a single form to assume two or more identities. Though it is found in older painting, like most of the Surrealist techniques, and traces of it appear in Cubist works, the double image was used most successfully by a late comer to Surrealism, Salvador Dali. Dali contributed to Surrealism a doctrine of "paranoiac-critical activity" which recommended that the artist emulate the state of mind of the victim of paranoia, whose obsession leads him to attribute strange and secret values to everyday objects and events. Many of Dali's paintings illustrate this duality. His "Paranoiac Face" shows some figures sitting in the sand before a dome-shaped hut with some trees in back of it. When the painting is turned on its side, these shapes form half of a terrified female face, the figures becoming shadows defining nose and lips, and the trees the hair. This technique is used with considerable virtuosity in "Endless Enigma," where a mountain suggests a man resting on his arm, a beam of wood is both the stem of a cello and the prow of a boat, and a group of objects, including a rock, a reflection in a stream, a boat, and the figure of a seated woman, unexpectedly take on the appearance of a face staring out of the canvas.

The Waste Land's principle of organization, which treats its subject by looking before and after rather than thinking precisely on the event, requires the constant presence of an ambiguity which is a strict counterpart of the device of the double image. Every episode, character, and symbol in the poem is transformed under the pressures of its context into something else, so that it possesses two identities, and often more, at once. Brooks has described Eliot's method in this way:

> The poet works in terms of surface parallelisms which in reality make ironical contrasts, and in terms of surface contrasts which in reality constitute parallelisms. . . . The two aspects taken together give the effect of chaotic experience ordered into a new whole, though the realistic surface of experience is faithfully retained.[3]

The effect of double image is achieved through ambiguous symbols, allusions, the exploitation of physical resemblances, and quotations which are made to fit new applications. Thus, Mr. Eugenides, because he is one-eyed, is also the merchant in the Tarot pack, and because he is half blind, has a certain relationship with Tiresias. In the lines

> A crowd flowed over London Bridge, so many,
> I had not thought death had undone so many,

ordinary twentieth century Londoners become a part of the mass of lost souls Dante sees on the great plain just within the gate of the Inferno. And in

> While I was fishing in the dull canal
> On a winter evening round behind the gashouse
> Musing upon the king my brother's wreck
> And on the king my father's death before him,

the speaker who is, according to the allusions, both Ferdinand of *The Tempest,* and the disabled Fisher King of the poem's central legend, is imprisoned in a dreary modern industrial city. A line from Spenser's "Prothalamion," "Sweet Thames, run softly till I end my song," appears in the description of the filth and desolation of the modern Thames, so that the comparatively undefiled river of an earlier time is recalled, and with it is expressed the contrast between the base

---

[3] Cleanth Brooks, "*The Waste Land:* Critique of the Myth," *reprinted in this volume, p. 59. —Ed.*

loves of which the modern river is the scene and the holy love celebrated in Spenser's poem.

Certainly the presence of corresponding innovations of method in
the productions of artists working in different media and having different philosophies suggests that there is a relationship between them,
in spite of the differences. It is the same sort of relationship as that
which justifies the application of the single term, "baroque" to Bach's
fugues, Milton's epics, and Tiepolo's paintings, or of the term "romantic" to Shelley's poems, Beethoven's symphonies, and Corot's
landscapes, a relationship based on general and elusive similarities
of style rather than content. Content expresses thought or feeling,
but style reflects the unconscious attitudes from which thought and
feeling emerge, and these in turn are conditioned by subtle and per-
vasive influences generally originating outside the arts. *The Waste
Land's* style exhibits a responsiveness to the experimentalist mood
of the avant-garde paintings of its time, a mood initiated by Cézanne's
distortions of color and perspective, and by Baudelaire's insistence on
the superiority of imaginative over imitative art. Like these paintings
also, *The Waste Land* pursues its theme in a way which reflects the
insights of contemporary pioneers in science and philosophy, whose
discoveries were simultaneously creating new knowledge and new mysteries. By striving for a more thorough understanding of psychic and
material phenomena and by demonstrating that the view of reality
yielded by common sense and surface appearance was deceptive, such
thinkers as Freud, Planck, Bergson, and Einstein were setting artists
an important example. Their work involved the revision of conventional ideas about such things as space, time, and personality, the
standards of evidence and relevance, and the force of intuitive and
analogical thinking. In *The Waste Land* and the paintings to which
it corresponds, we witness a parallel attempt to achieve an unprecedented completeness and penetration of vision by the use of new
methods. Just as the Cubists, reacting against the superficiality of
Impressionism, sought greater completeness by stressing form and volume, Eliot, reacting against the unsupported emotionalism of Tennyson and the Georgian poets, sought it by employing history, irony,
contrasts, and realism. It is clear that *The Waste Land,* in spite of its
affinity with older traditions, participated fully in the broad revolution of sensibility represented by the experimental paintings. Eliot
and the painters we have mentioned may say different things about
the spiritual problems of their time, but they speak the same language, an idiom coined from the scientific and philosophic contribu-
tions of the early twentieth century.

T. S. Eliot as the International Hero

by Delmore Schwartz

A culture hero is one who brings new arts and skills to mankind. Prometheus was a culture hero and the inventors of the radio may also be said to be culture heroes, although this is hardly to be confounded with the culture made available by the radio.

The inventors of the radio made possible a new range of experience. This is true of certain authors; for example, it is true of Wordsworth in regard to nature, and Proust in regard to time. It is not true of Shakespeare, but by contrast it is true of Surrey and the early Elizabethan playwrights who invented blank verse. Thus the most important authors are not always culture heroes, and thus no rank, stature, or scope is of necessity implicit in speaking of the author as a culture hero.

When we speak of nature and of a new range of experience, we may think of a mountain range: some may make the vehicles by means of which a mountain is climbed, some may climb the mountain, and some may apprehend the new view of the surrounding countryside which becomes possible from the heights of the mountain. T. S. Eliot is a culture hero in each of these three ways. This becomes clear when we study the relationship of his work to the possible experiences of modern life. The term *possible* should be kept in mind, for many human beings obviously disregard and turn their backs upon much of modern life, although modern life does not in the least cease to circumscribe and penetrate their existence.

The reader of T. S. Eliot by turning the dials of his radio can hear the capitals of the world, London, Vienna, Athens, Alexandria, Jerusalem. What he hears will be news of the agony of war. Both the agony and the width of this experience are vivid examples of how the poetry of T. S. Eliot has a direct relationship to modern life. The width and the height and the depth of modern life are exhibited in his poetry; the agony and the horror of modern life are represented

Delmore Schwartz, "T. S. Eliot as the International Hero," Partisan Review, XII: 2 (Spring 1945), 199–206. Copyright © 1945, by Partisan Review. Reprinted by permission of the Partisan Review and the Estate of Delmore Schwartz.

as inevitable to any human being who does not wish to deceive himself with systematic lies. Thus it is truly significant that E. M. Forster, in writing of Eliot, should recall August 1914 and the beginning of the First World War; it is just as significant that he should speak of first reading Eliot's poems in Alexandria, Egypt, during that war, and that he should conclude by saying that Eliot was one who had looked into the abyss and refused henceforward to deny or forget the fact.

We are given an early view of the international hero in the quasi-autobiographical poem which Eliot entitles: "Mélange Adultère De Tout." The title, borrowed from a poem by Corbière, is ironic, but the adulterous mixture of practically everything, every time and every place, is not ironic in the least: a teacher in America, the poem goes, a journalist in England, a lecturer in Yorkshire, a literary nihilist in Paris, overexcited by philosophy in Germany, a wanderer from Omaha to Damascus, he has celebrated, he says, his birthday at an African oasis, dressed in a giraffe's skin. Let us place next to this array another list of names and events as heterogeneous as a circus or America itself: St. Louis, New England, Boston, Harvard, England, Paris, the First World War, Oxford, London, the Russian Revolution, the Church of England, the postwar period, the world crisis and depression, the Munich Pact, and the Second World War. If this list seems farfetched or forced, if it seems that such a list might be made for any author, the answer is that these names and events are *presences* in Eliot's work in a way which is not true of many authors, good and bad, who have lived through the same years.

Philip Rahv has shown how the heroine of Henry James is best understood as the heiress of all the ages. So, in a further sense, the true protagonist of Eliot's poems is the heir of all the ages. He is the descendant of the essential characters of James in that he is the American who visits Europe with a Baedeker in his hand, just like Isabel Archer. But the further sense in which he is the heir of all the ages is illustrated when Eliot describes the seduction of a typist in a London flat from the point of view of Tiresias, a character in a play by Sophocles. To suppose that this is the mere exhibition of learning or reading is a banal misunderstanding. The important point is that the presence of Tiresias illuminates the seduction of the typist just as much as a description of her room. Hence Eliot writes in his notes to *The Waste Land* that "what Tiresias *sees* is the substance of the poem." The illumination of the ages is available at any moment, and when the typist's indifference and boredom in the act of love must be represented, it is possible for Eliot to invoke and paraphrase a lyric from a play by Oliver Goldsmith. Literary allusion has become not merely a Miltonic reference to Greek gods and Old Testament geography, not merely the citation of parallels, but a powerful and inevitable habit of mind, a habit which issues in judgment and the representation of different levels of experience, past and present.

James supposed that his theme was the international theme: would it not be more precise to speak of it as the transatlantic theme? This effort at a greater exactness defines what is involved in Eliot's work. Henry James was concerned with the American in Europe. Eliot cannot help but be concerned with the whole world and all history. Tiresias sees the nature of love in all times and all places and when Sweeney outwits a scheming whore, the fate of Agamemnon becomes relevant. So too, in the same way exactly, Eliot must recognize and use a correspondence between St. Augustine and Buddha in speaking of sensuality. And thus, as he writes again in his notes to *The Waste Land,* "The collocation of these two representatives of eastern and western asceticism as the culmination of this part of the poem is not an accident." And it is not an accident that the international hero should have come from St. Louis, Missouri, or at any rate from America. Only an American with a mind and sensibility which is cosmopolitan and expatriated could have seen Europe as it is seen in *The Waste Land.*

A literary work may be important in many ways, but surely one of the ways in which it is important is in its relationship to some important human interest or need, or in its relationship to some new aspect of human existence. Eliot's work is important in relationship to the fact that experience has become international. We have become an international people, and hence an international hero is possible. Just as the war is international, so the true causes of many of the things in our lives are worldwide, and we are able to understand the character of our lives only when we are aware of all history, of the philosophy of history, of primitive peoples and the Russian Revolution, of ancient Egypt and the unconscious mind. Thus again it is no accident that in *The Waste Land* use is made of *The Golden Bough,* and a book on the quest of the Grail; and the way in which images and associations appear in the poem illustrates a new view of consciousness, the depths of consciousness and the unconscious mind.

The protagonist of *The Waste Land* stands on the banks of the Thames and quotes the Upanishads, and this very quotation, the command to "give, sympathize, and control," makes possible a comprehensive insight into the difficulty of his life in the present. But this emphasis upon one poem of Eliot's may be misleading. What is true of much of his poetry is also true of his criticism. When the critic writes of tradition and the individual talent, when he declares the necessity for the author of a consciousness of the past as far back as Homer, when he brings the reader back to Dante, the Elizabethans and Andrew Marvell, he is also speaking as the heir of all the ages.

The emphasis on a consciousness of literature may also be misleading, for nowhere better than in Eliot can we see the difference between being merely literary and making the knowedge of literature an element in vision, that is to say, an essential part of the process of seeing anything and everything. Thus, to cite the advent of Tiresias again, the literary character of his appearance is matched by the unliterary actuality by means of which he refers to himself as being "like a taxi throbbing waiting." In one way, the subject of *The Waste Land* is the sensibility of the protagonist, a sensibility which is literary, philosophical, cosmopolitan and expatriated. But this sensibility is concerned not with itself as such, but with the common things of modern life, with two such important aspects of existence as religious belief and making love. To summon to mind such profound witnesses as Freud and D. H. Lawrence is to remember how often, in modern life, love has been the worst sickness of human beings.

The extent to which Eliot's poetry is directly concerned with love is matched only by the extent to which it is concerned with religious belief and the crisis of moral values. J. Alfred Prufrock is unable to make love to women of his own class and kind because of shyness, self-consciousness, and fear of rejection. The protagonists of other poems in Eliot's first book are men or women laughed at or rejected in love, and a girl deserted by her lover seems like a body deserted by the soul.

In Eliot's second volume of poems, an old man's despair issues in part from his inability to make love, while Sweeney, an antithetical character, is able to make love, but is unable to satisfy the woman with whom he copulates. In *The Waste Land,* the theme of love as a failure is again uppermost. Two lovers return from a garden after a moment of love, and the woman is overcome by despair or pathological despondency. A lady, perhaps the same woman who has returned from the garden in despair, becomes hysterical in her boudoir because her lover or her husband has nothing to say to her and cannot give her life any meaning or interest: "What shall I do now?" she says, "what shall I ever do?" The neurasthenic lady is succeeded in the poem by cockney women who gossip about another cockney

woman who has been made ill by contraceptive pills taken to avoid
the consequences of love; which is to say that the sickness of love has
struck down every class in society: "What you get married for, if
you don't want children?" And then we witness the seduction of the
typist; and then other aspects of the sickness of love appear when,
on the Thames bank, three girls ruined by love rehearse the sins of
the young men with whom they have been having affairs. In the last
part of the poem, the impossibility of love, the gulf between one
human being and another, is the answer to the command to give,
that is to say, to give oneself or surrender oneself to another human
being in the act of making love.

Elsewhere love either results in impotence, or it is merely copulation. In "The Hollow Men," the hollow men are incapable of making love because there is a shadow which falls between the desire
and the spasm. The kinship of love and belief is affirmed when the
difficulty of love and of religious belief are expressed in the same
way and as parallels, by means of a paraphrase and parody of the
Lord's Prayer. In "Sweeney Agonistes," Sweeney returns to say that
there is nothing in love but copulation, which, like birth and death,
is boring. Sweeney's boredom should be placed in contrast with the
experience of Burbank, who encountered the Princess Volupine in
Venice, and found himself impotent with her. A comparison ought
also to be made between Sweeney and the protagonist of one of
Eliot's poems in French who harks back to a childhood experience
of love: "I tickled her to make her laugh. I experienced a moment
of power and delirium." Eliot's characters when they make love
either suffer from what the psychoanalysts term "psychic impotence,"
or they make love so inadequately that the lady is left either hysterical
or indifferent when the episode is over. The characters who are
potent and insensitive are placed in contrast with the characters who
are impotent and sensitive. Grishkin has a bust which promises pneu-
matic bliss, while Burbank's kind, the kind of a man who goes to
Europe with a Baedeker, has to crawl between the dry ribs of meta-
physics because no contact possible to flesh is satisfactory. The potent
and the insensitive, such as Sweeney, are not taken in by the ladies,
the nightingales and the whores; but Burbank, like Agamemnon, is
betrayed and undone.

This synoptic recitation might be increased by many more examples. Its essence is expressed perfectly in "Little Gidding": "Love
is the unfamiliar name." But we ought to remember that the difficulty
of making love, that is to say, of entering into the most intimate of
relationships, is not the beginning but the consequence of the whole

character of modern life. That is why the apparatus of reference which the poet brings to bear upon failure in love involves all history ("And I Tiresias have foresuffered all") and is international. So too the old man who is the protagonist of "Gerontion" must refer to human beings of many nationalities, to Mr. Silvero at Limoges, Hakagawa, Madame de Tornquist, Fräulein von Kulp, and Christ (the tiger), and he finds it necessary to speak of all history as well as his failure in love. History is made to illuminate love and love is made to illuminate history. In modern life, human beings are whirled beyond the circuit of the constellations: their intimate plight is seen in connection or relation with the anguish of the Apostles after Calvary, the murder of Agamemnon, the insanity of Ophelia, and children who chant that London bridge is falling down. In the same way, the plight of Prufrock is illuminated by means of a rich, passing reference to Michelangelo, the sculptor of the strong and heroic man. Only when the poet is the heir of all the ages can he make significant use of so many different and distant kinds of experience. But conversely, only when experience becomes international, only when many different and distant kinds of experience are encountered by the poet, does he find it necessary to become the heir of all the ages.

Difficulty in love is inseparable from the deracination and the alienation from which the international man suffers. When the traditional beliefs, sanctions, and bonds of the community and of the family decay or disappear in the distance like a receding harbor, then love ceases to be an act which is in relation to the life of the community, and in immediate relation to the family and other human beings. Love becomes purely personal. It is isolated from the past and the future, and since it is isolated from all other relationships, since it is no longer celebrated, evaluated, and given a status by the community, love does become merely copulation. The protagonist of "Gerontion" uses one of the most significant phrases in Eliot's work when he speaks of himself as living in a *rented* house; which is to say, not in the house where his forebears lived. He lives in a rented house, he is unable to make love, and he knows that history has many cunning, deceptive, and empty corridors. The nature of the house, of love, and of history are interdependent aspects of modern life.

When we compare Eliot's poetry to the poetry of Valèry, Yeats, and Rilke, Eliot's direct and comprehensive concern with the essential nature of modern life gains an external definition. Yeats writes of Leda and he writes of the nature of history; Valèry writes of Narcissus and the serpent in the Garden of Eden; Rilke is inspired by great works of art, by Christ's mother, and by Orpheus. Yet in each of these authors the subject is transformed into a timeless essence. The heritage of Western culture is available to these authors and they use it in many beautiful ways; but the fate of Western culture and the historical sense as such does not become an important part of their poetry. And then if we compare Eliot with Auden and with Pound, a further definition becomes clear. In his early work, Auden is inspired by an international crisis in a social and political sense; in his new work, he writes as a teacher and preacher and secular theologian. In neither period is all history and all culture a necessary part of the subject or the sensibility which is dealing with the subject. With Pound, we come closer to Eliot and the closeness sharpens the difference. Pound is an American in Europe too, and Pound, not Eliot, was the first to grasp the historical and international dimension of experience, as we can see in an early effort of his to explain the method of the *Cantos* and the internal structure of each *Canto:* "All times are contemporaneous," he wrote, and in the *Cantos,* he attempts to deal with all history as if it were part of the present. But he fails; he remains for the most part an American in Europe, and the *Cantos* are never more than a book of souvenirs of a tour of the world and a tour of culture.

To be international is to be a citizen of the world and thus a citizen of no particular city. The world as such is not a community and it has no constitution or government: it is the turning world in which the human being, surrounded by the consequences of all times and all places, must live his life as a human being and not as the citizen of any nation. Hence, to be the heir of all the ages is to inherit nothing but a consciousness of how all heirlooms are rooted in the past. Dominated by the historical consciousness, the international hero finds that all beliefs affect the holding of any belief (he cannot think of Christianity without remembering Adonis); he finds that many languages affect each use of speech (*The Waste Land* concludes with a passage in four languages).

When nationalism attempts to renew itself, it can do so only through the throes of war. And when nationalism in America attempts to become articulate, when a poet like Carl Sandburg writes that "The past is a bucket of ashes," or when Henry Ford makes the purely American remark that "History is the bunk," we have only to remember such a pilgrimage as that of Ford in the Peace Ship in which he attempted to bring the First World War to an end in order to see that anyone can say whatever he likes: no matter what anyone says, existence has become international for everyone.

Eliot's political and religious affirmations are at another extreme, and they do not resemble Ford's quixotic pilgrimage except as illustrating the starting-point of the modern American, and his inevitable journey to Europe. What should be made explicit here is that only one who has known fully the deracination and alienation inherent in modern life can be moved to make so extreme an effort at returning to the traditional community as Eliot makes in attaching himself to Anglo-Catholicism and Royalism. Coming back may well be the same thing as going away; or at any rate, the effort to return home may exhibit the same predicament and the same topography as the fact of departure. Only by going to Europe, by crossing the Atlantic and living thousands of miles from home, does the international hero conceive of the complex nature of going home.

Modern life may be compared to a foreign country in which a foreign language is spoken. Eliot is the international hero because he has made the journey to the foreign country and described the nature of the new life in the foreign country. Since the future is bound to be international, if it is anything at all, we are all the bankrupt heirs of the ages, and the moments of the crisis expressed in Eliot's work are a prophecy of the crises of our own future in regard to love, religious belief, good and evil, the good life, and the nature of the just society. *The Waste Land* will soon be as good as new.

Chronology of Important Dates

T. S. Eliot	*World Events*
1910 In Paris, attending the lectures of Henri Bergson at the University of Paris. (1910–11).	B. Russell and A. N. Whitehead, *Principia Mathematica,* Marie Curie, *Treatise on Radiology,* and "Futurist Manifesto" published.
1911 Resumes graduate work at Harvard in Sanskrit and Oriental philosophy. Traveling fellowship in Germany in 1914 interrupted by war.	A. Schönberg's manual of harmony expounds the twelve-tone scale. Rilke's *Duino Elegies* published.
1914 Settles in London, begins close friendship with Ezra Pound.	Outbreak of World War I. Completion by Sir J. G. Frazer of *The Golden Bough,* begun in 1890.
1917 *Prufrock and Other Observations* published.	U. S. declares war on Germany in April. Jung publishes *The Unconscious;* first use of term "surrealist" applied to Picasso.
1921 Winter: Begins *The Waste Land.*	Beginnings of economic depression throughout Europe. Picasso's *Three Musicians,* Prokofiev's *Love for Three Oranges.*
1922 February: Pound mentions having seen Eliot's early version of *The Waste Land.*	James Joyce's *Ulysses* published. In October, Mussolini marches on Rome and forms a Fascist government.
1922 October: *The Waste Land* published in *The Criterion,* a magazine edited anonymously by Eliot.	Igor Stravinsky's *Mavra.* Death of Marcel Proust.
1922 November: *The Waste Land* published in *The Dial.*	
1922 December 15: *The Waste Land* published by Boni and Liveright, with "Notes," in an edition of 1,000 copies.	

	T. S. Eliot	*World Events*
1922	*The Waste Land* wins *The Dial* award of $2,000.	
1923	September 12: *The Waste Land* published by Leonard and Virginia Woolf's Hogarth Press, in an edition of 460 copies.	F. Scott Fitzgerald, *Tales of the Jazz Age* published.
1924		Nikolai Lenin, Woodrow Wilson, Joseph Conrad, and F. H. Bradley die.
1927	Eliot becomes a British citizen and a member of the Anglican Church.	
1929		October: Wall Street crash in U. S.
1930	*Ash-Wednesday* published.	March 2: Death of D. H. Lawrence.
1933		January 30: Hitler appointed Chancellor of Germany.
1935	*Murder in the Cathedral* performed.	Stravinsky's ballet *Game of Cards*.
1936		Dylan Thomas, *Twenty-five Poems*. Criticism of works of art, literature, and music is forbidden in Germany. May 8: O. Spengler dies.
1937		Picasso's *Guernica*. Christopher Cauldwell, *Illusion and Reality*, B. Brecht, *A Penny for the Poor*, J. P. Sartre, *Nausée* published.
1939	*The Family Reunion* performed.	Italy invades Albania, Franco is victorious in Spain, Germany invades Poland: World War II begins.
1943	*The Four Quartets* completed. (1936–43).	Jacques Maritain, *Christianity and Democracy*.

T. S. Eliot   *World Events*

1945		August 6, 9: Atomic bombs dropped on Hiroshima and Nagasaki. M. Buber, *For The Sake Of Heaven*. M. Chagall, sets and costumes for *The Firebird*.
1948	Eliot awarded Nobel Prize and Order of Merit.	
1960	Eliot prepares an autograph fair copy of *The Waste Land,* adding a new line.	
1961	Faber and Faber publishes an edition of 300 copies of a text of *The Waste Land* authorized by T. S. Eliot.	
1965	January 4: Eliot dies.	January 24: Death of Sir Winston Churchill. March 7: Violence breaks out in Selma, Alabama. March 8: U. S. Marines land in South Vietnam. The Beatles awarded M.B.E. in Queen's Birthday Honors. September 4: Death of Albert Schweitzer.

Notes on the Editor and Contributors

JAY MARTIN, the editor of this volume, is Associate Professor of English and American Studies at Yale University, and the author of works on Conrad Aiken and *Harvests of Change: American Literature, 1865-1914*. He is currently working on a biography of Nathanael West.

CONRAD AIKEN, a contemporary and friend of Eliot's, has written distinguished poetry, fiction, and criticism, as well as an autobiography, *Ushant*, in which he writes of his friendship with Eliot.

CLEANTH BROOKS, Gray Professor of Rhetoric at Yale University, is the author of many books on English and American literature, including *William Faulkner: The Yoknapatawpha Country*.

R. G. COLLINGWOOD, British philosopher, wrote several important books on aesthetics, including *Principles of Art*. He died in 1943.

DAVID C. FOWLER is a Professor of English at the University of Washington. He is well-known for his studies of *Piers Plowman* and medieval literature.

MORRIS FREEDMAN, Professor of English at the University of New Mexico and formerly an associate editor of *Commentary*, has written widely on both Milton and American literature.

WILLIAM M. GIBSON, co-editor of the *Mark Twain-Howells Letters*, is a Professor of English at New York University.

HERBERT HOWARTH teaches at the University of Manitoba. He has written numerous magazine articles and is the author of *The Irish Writers, 1880–1940*.

HUGH KENNER, editor of *T. S. Eliot: A Collection of Critical Essays*, has also written books on Ezra Pound and Wyndham Lewis. He is a Professor of English at the University of California (Santa Barbara).

JACOB KORG has written frequently on Victorian and contemporary literature, including a biography of George Gissing. He is a Professor of English at the University of Washington.

BRUCE R. MCELDERRY, Professor of English at the University of Southern California, has written on Romantic, Victorian, and American literature.

WILLIAM T. MOYNIHAN, author of *The Craft and Art of Dylan Thomas,* is a Professor of English at the University of Connecticut.

ROY HARVEY PEARCE, Professor of English at the University of California (San Diego) has written importantly of 19th and 20th century American poetry.

B. RAJAN, Indian critic and novelist, is Professor of English at the University of Windsor, Ontario, Canada.

JOHN CROWE RANSOM. Formerly editor of *The Kenyon Review,* poet and critic, Ransom has had an important influence on contemporary literature.

I. A. RICHARDS, English critic, is the author of many volumes of criticism, including *Principles of Literary Criticism, Science and Poetry,* and *Practical Criticism.*

DELMORE SCHWARTZ. A well-known poet, he also wrote many important critical reviews and essays on contemporary poets, and was an editor of the *Partisan Review* during 1943–1955.

STEPHEN SPENDER first became famous as a poet in the 1930's, but has also written important criticism and fiction.

ALLEN TATE, the distinguished poet and critic, is a Professor of English at the University of Minnesota. His *Collected Essays* was published in 1959.

ERIC THOMPSON is a Professor of English at Ohio University.

JOHN B. VICKERY teaches at the University of California (Riverside), and writes on modern literature.

GEORGE T. WRIGHT teaches English literature at the University of Tennessee and writes on modern poetry, fiction, and literary theory.

Selected Bibliography

Bacon, Helen, "The Sibyl in the Bottle," *Virginia Quarterly Review*, XXXIV (1958), 262–76. [A careful study of the implications for the poem of Eliot's epigraph.]

Bowra, C. M., *The Creative Experiment*, London, 1949, pp. 159–88. [One of the best discussions of the style, symbolism, and modernity of Eliot's poem.]

Day, Robert, " 'City Man' in *The Waste Land*," *PMLA*, LXXX (1965), 285–91. [A discussion of Eliot's use of actual scenes in London and of the city as a symbol.]

Drew, Elizabeth, *T. S. Eliot: The Design of His Poetry*, New York, 1949, pp. 58–90. [A discussion of the poem from the viewpoint of Jungian myth criticism.]

Explicator, vols. VI–XXIV (1948–1965).
For explications of particular passages in *The Waste Land*, see the following: Albert Cook, "III, ll. 262–65," VI, #7; Eleanor M. Sickels, "A Game of Chess," VII, #20; Lysander Kemp, "I, 49–50," VII, #60; Lyle Glazier, "I, 24–30," VIII, #26; Lysander Kemp, "I, 43–59," VIII, #27; Eleanor M. Sickels, "I, 24–30," IX, #4; Lyman A. Cotten, "I, 43–46," IX, #7; Ray Smith, "I, 74–75," IX, #9; W. T. Weathers, "I, 24–30," IX, #31; Harry M. Schwalb, "A Game of Chess," XI, #46; John Ross Baker, "ll. 77–93," XIV, #27; William H. Marshall, "l. 182," XVII, #42; Rene Forten, "ll. 207–14," XXI, #32; James O. Merritt, "ll. 74–75," XXIII, #31; Herbert Knust, "l. 74," XXIII, #74; Dale Kramer, "ll. 392–95," XXIV, #74. [These explications, the reader should be warned, vary greatly in quality.]

Gardner, Helen, *The Art of T. S. Eliot*, New York, 1950, pp. 84–98. [Excellent commentary on several aspects of the poem.]

Leavis, F. R., "The Waste Land," *New Bearings in English Poetry*, London, 1932, pp. 112–32. [A pioneering essay which has influenced most later discussion, and is still useful.]

Nelson, Armour H., "The Critics and *The Waste Land*, 1922–1949," *English Studies*, XXXVI (1955), 1–15. [Useful as a summary of commentary on the poem, and as a bibliographical guide.]

111

Rai, Vikramaditya, *The Waste Land: A Critical Study,* Varanasi, India, 1965. [The only book-length study of the poem; relates Eliot to oriental philosophy.]

Smith, Grover C., *T. S. Eliot's Poetry and Plays,* Chicago, 1956, pp. 72–98. [The chapter on *The Waste Land,* in this general book, is an especially good guide to the sources of the poem.]

Tate, Allen, ed., *T. S. Eliot: The Man and His Work,* New York, 1967. Originally *Sewanee Review,* LXXIV (1966). [Most of the essays in this memorial volume deal generally with Eliot's work; there are many useful comments throughout.]

Unger, Leonard, ed., *T. S. Eliot: A Selected Critique,* New York, 1948. [A basic collection of essays on all aspects of Eliot's career. See the especially useful essays by E. M. Forster, pp. 11–17; Paul Elmer More, pp. 24–29; Malcolm Cowley, pp. 30–33; Yvor Winters, pp. 75–113; R. P. Blackmur, pp. 236–62; Allen Tate, pp. 289–95; and Louis L. Martz, pp. 444–62.]

Williamson, George, *Reader's Guide to T. S. Eliot,* New York, 1957, pp. 115–54. [A full-scale attempt at explication of the poem.]

Woodward, Daniel, "Notes on the Publishing History and Text of *The Waste Land,*" *Papers of the Bibliographical Society of America,* LVIII (1964), 252–69. [Interesting discussion of the text of the poem.]

TWENTIETH CENTURY VIEWS

American Authors

TWENTIETH CENTURY VIEWS

British Authors

TWENTIETH CENTURY VIEWS

European Authors

RODMAN PUBLIC LIBRARY
215 East Broadway
Alliance, OH 44601